C000234109

GATE BIENNALE

Sugar Dollies
Klaus Chatten
Translation by Anthony Vivis

After the Rain
Sergi Belbel
Translation by Xavier Rodríguez Rosell, David George and John London

Methuen Fast Track Playscripts

First published in Great Britain 1996
by Methuen Drama
an imprint of Reed International Books Ltd
Michelin House, 81 Fulham Road, London SW3 6RB
and Auckland, Melbourne, Singapore and Toronto
in association with the Gate Theatre
11 Pembridge Road, London W11 3HQ

Sugar Dollies translation copyright © 1996 by Anthony Vivis
After the Rain translation copyright © 1996 by Xavier
Rodríguez Rosell, David George and John London

The authors and translators have asserted their moral rights

ISBN 0 413 70790 3

A CIP catalogue record for this book is available from the
British Library

Typeset by Wilmaset Ltd, Birkenhead, Wirral

Printed in Great Britain by Cox & Wyman Ltd, Reading,
Berkshire

Caution

All rights in these plays are strictly reserved and application
for performance etc. should be made to: *Sugar Dollies*,
Rosica Colin Ltd, 1 Clareville Grove Mews, London SW7
5AH; *After the Rain*, John London, 14 Leigh Street, London
WC1H 9EW. No performance may be given unless a licence
has been obtained.

This paperback is sold subject to the condition that it shall
not, by way of trade or otherwise, be lent, resold, hired out,
or otherwise circulated without the publisher's prior consent
in any form of binding or cover other than that in which it is
published and without a similar condition being imposed on
the subsequent purchaser.

GATE BIENNALE
A CELEBRATION OF CONTEMPORARY EUROPEAN THEATRE AT THE GATE THEATRE

Gate Biennale is a unique celebration of contemporary European writing and writers. Based on a European model this is a British first, a biennial festival of the newest, freshest work from our continent. The Gate has spent considerable time researching the most exciting European playwrights and their plays from 1993 to 1995 and the season presents work from the United Kingdom, Austria, Sweden, Russia, Germany and Spain.

The emphasis of the festival is on the writers, all of whom we believe will come to dominate European theatrical culture over the next twenty years. Gate Biennale reveals the energy and wit shared by a generation with all six plays casting a scathing eye over contemporary Europe. The writers are political, scabrous and very funny.

After presenting plays from Britain, Austria, Sweden and Russia the celebration of new European writing ends with two plays juxtaposing Germany and Spain. Two writers born in the same year but to different cultural backgrounds; we present Klaus Chatten's **Sugar Dollies** and Sergi Belbel's **After the Rain.**

Taking Molière as his major influence, Chatten emulates his dark depiction of human nature in a theatre stripped bare of any formality and making actors the centre of the piece. Although his humour dips to the blackest pitch of despair, his ability to capture the state of the nation in carefully constructed characters and invest his plays with glimmers of hope, has led to his plays becoming instant successes. His first play, **Unser Dorf soll Schöner Werden** (1993), went straight from the National stage to being performed in most of Germany's regional theatres. **Prunksitzung** (**Sugar Dollies**, 1995), a murderish yet vibrant comedy, receives its world premiere at the Gate before opening at the Deutsches Theater, Berlin, in June 1996.

Belbel's work concentrates on personal relationships and the treatment of sexuality, often 'deviant', within them. He is considered the saviour of Catalan text-based drama, although ironically not actually born to a Catalan family. At 32, he is fast becoming not only the star of Catalan writing but of Spanish theatre with plays such as **After the Rain** and **Caresses** performed to huge acclaim. 'His commitment is not to the audience, but to himself, to his project of theatrical creation, which, for the moment, refuses to make any concession to audiences.' *Contemporary Catalan Theatre: An Introduction*

Gate Biennale will offer London a chance to see some varied and radical work as well as breathing life back into theatrical debate. The festival is designed to ask important questions about Britain's European identity, as well as if there is such a thing as a general European identity, at a time when the issue has never been more sensitive; but it is also a celebration, diverse and chaotic, of the most innovative contemporary work and writers in Europe today.

Acknowledgements

Gate Biennale was funded by:
The International Initiatives Fund of the Arts Council of England
The European Cultural Foundation, which promotes European cultural co-operation by running a grants programme, developing new projects and programmes in priority areas and serving as the centre of a network of fourteen independent institutes and centres for research and study
The Visiting Arts of Great Britain

Gate Biennale was made possible by the generous support of the following organisations and individuals: The Cultural Relations Department of the Foreign and Commonwealth Office, BBC World Service, Jenny Hall, The Jerwood Foundation, London Arts Board, Allied Domecq, and the Arthur Andersen Foundation, the Swedish Embassy and the Goethe Institute. Methuen Drama will publish all the plays in the season.

With thanks to:
David Pike, Bruce McAlpine, Margaret Saville, Laura Hacker, Sue Higginson, Ian Oag, Damaso de Lario, Silvia Griffiths, Henrika Hawkins, photographer Pam Ross, Terry's London Trunk Store and Farringdon Locksmiths.

The Gate

The Gate exists to introduce the work of international playwrights to a British audience. Its acclaimed seasons of work – including Women in World Theatre, The Spanish Golden Age, Six Plays for

Europe, Agamemnon's Children and Storm and Stress – have led to a number of awards and widespread acclaim.

Now in its sixteenth year, the Gate has always aspired to produce the best of undiscovered world drama, providing a platform for the emerging talents of actors, designers, directors and translators. The permanent staff earn less than a living wage. All the actors, directors, designers and stage managers work for expenses only. The Gate survives because of their energy, commitment, talent and dedication to work. We constantly work towards achieving public funding. If you enjoy the Gate's work and would like to ensure its survival into the future, then please join our Friend's scheme.

Gate Theatre Awards

1990 LWT Plays on Stage Award for *Damned for Despair*
1990 Time Out Award for Consummate Classics Season
1991 Prudential Award for Theatre
1991 EC Platform Europe Award
1991 Peter Brook/Empty Space Award for the *Ingolstadt* Plays
1991 Time Out Award for the Directors of the *Ingolstadt* Plays
1991 Plays and Players Awards for Best Director and Best Production of *Damned for Despair*
1992 Time Out Award for Best Designer on *Damned for Despair*
1992 Olivier Award for Outstanding Achievement
1992 LWT Plays on Stage Award for *Bohemian Lights*
1993 International Theatre Institute Award for Excellence in International Theatre
1993 Time Out Award for Best Director/Designer of *Elisabeth II*
1994 Peter Brook/Empty Space Award for the Expansion of the Theatre
1994 Time Out Award for Best Designer on *The Great Highway*
1995 Peter Brook/Empty Space Award Special Mention
1996 Guinness Ingenuity Award for Pub Theatre

Karabé Award – Jenny Hall

The Karabé award is a unique one-year Associate Director bursary sponsored by Jenny Hall who is a long-time patron of the Gate, to provide a young, innovative director the opportunity of working closely with the Gate Theatre. The winner directs at least one full-scale production at the Gate and is involved in all aspects of the development and day to day running of the theatre.

1995 Indhu Rubasingham (runner up Pat Kiernan)
1994 David Farr

Board of Directors

Mark Bayley
Kevin Cahill (Chairman)
Rupert Christiansen
Roderick Hall
Jonathan Hull
Lucy Parker
Lucy Stout

Friends of the Gate Scheme

Please take a form available at the box office.

Friends of the Gate £20+

- Your name is automatically added to our mailing list
- Priority ticket booking
- Two tickets for the price of one for the first week of all Gate productions
- Invitation to special events including the Annual Friends Lunch

Honoured Friend £150+

- All the benefits of being a Friend plus
- Listings in every programme for the year of subscription
- Reserved seating

Hero £500+

- All the benefits of being an Honoured Friend plus
- Annual thank you in a national newspaper
- Inclusion on the Heroes Board in the Gate foyer

Giving a donation

Donations of £250.00 and over are eligible for Giftaid; the scheme, operated by the Inland Revenue, enables the charity to increase the donation by a third of its value. Please call the Gate on 0171 229 5387 for more details.

Free Mailing list

To receive regular information about the Gate's unique seasons of international work, join our free mailing list – please fill in the form at the box office.

**The Gate Theatre presents
the World Premiere of**

Sugar Dollies

by Klaus Chatten

translated by Anthony Vivas

cast

Tabea	Nina Conti
Viola	Suzan Crowley
Peterchen	Rose Keegan
Rosy	Katrina Levon
Babette	Linda Broughton

Director	Indhu Rubasingham
Designer	Rosa Maggiora
Production Manager	Vian Curtis
Stage Manager	David Warwick
Deputy Stage Manager	Charlotte Hall
Assistant Designer	Caroline Grebbell

for the Biennale

Artistic Director	David Farr
Producer	Rose Garnett
Project Co-ordinator	Clare Goddard
Manager	Karen Hopkins
Literary Supervisor	Joy Lo Dico
Production Co-ordinator	Melissa Naylor
Press Officer	Rachel Stafford

Sugar Dollies is generously supported by the Goethe Institute

Indhu Rubasingham was the winner of the 1995 Karabé Award donated by Jenny Hall.

Biographies

Linda Broughton (Babette)
Theatre includes **Forty Years On** (Northcott Theatre, Exeter),
My Mother Said I Never Should (Theatre Royal,
Northampton), **Rookery Nook** (Greenwich), **Small Poppies**
(Young Vic), **When The Wind Blows** and **Macbeth** (Crucible
Sheffield), **Caucasian Chalk Circle** (Birmingham Rep).
Television includes **Hetty Wainthrop Investigates**, and **Fist of
Fun** (BBC), **The Bill** and **Ghost Watch** (Thames), **Wycliffe**
(ITV), **Expert Witness** and **Johnny and the Dead** (LWT),
Chandler and Co (Skreba Films), **Roughnecks** (First Choice
Productions) and **A Dark Adapted Eye** (Central Films).

Klaus Chatten (Writer)
After a full career as an actor and director working from Hamburg
to Moscow to New York, Klaus turned his hand to writing in 1993.
His first play, **Unser Dorf soll Schöner Werden**, premiered at
the Deutsches Theater, Berlin, to critical and popular acclaim. It
went on to be performed in most major regional theatres. He was the
first winner of the Playwright Competition Workshop at the
Literary Colloquium, Berlin, in 1994. In the same year, **Wir Legen
von Madagaskar** opened at the Bremer Theater and his film
script, **Silent Night** was directed by Dani Levy. The following year
he was awarded the Alfred Döblin Scholarship by the Academy of
Arts, Berlin. **Sugar Dollies** is receiving its world premiere at the
Gate and will open at the Deutsches Theater, Berlin, in June 1996.

Nina Conti (Tabea)
Bachelor of Arts with Honours in Philosophy, University of East
Anglia. Theatre includes **The Young Pretender** (Borders Festival
'95), Adele in **Shakers**, lead in **The Prime of Miss Jean Brodie**,
Arminta in **The Philanthropist**, Miss Prism in **The Importance
of Being Earnest**, Lady Chiltern in **An Ideal Husband**, Alithea
in **The Country Wife** and Mrs Webb in **Our Town**.

Suzan Crowley (Viola)
Began acting with National Youth Theatre then trained at the
Bristol Old Vic. Theatre work includes shows at the Glasgow
Citizens, Liverpool Playhouse and Everyman, where she worked
with Ken Campbell on the 10-play cycle, **The Warp**, playing 34
characters from a 13-year-old school boy to an 80-year-old tramp.
Television includes Dennis Potter's **Christabel**, Nicky Lucas in
The Knock and most recently the Machievellian DCI Helen

Chivers in **Backup**. Film includes **Born of Fire** and **The Draughtsman's Contract**.

Vian Curtis (Production Manager)
Resident Production Manager at the Gate. Trained at RADA.
Theatre includes **Bloodknot**, **Don Juan Comes Back From the War** (Gate), **Heart and Sole** (Gilded Balloon/Newcastle Comedy Festival), **So You Think You're Funny?!** (Gilded Balloon), **The Lottery Ticket** (BAC/Pleasance), carpenter for Hilton Productions and **Miss Julie** (New End Theatre, Hampstead).

Caroline Grebbell (Assistant Designer)
Work includes stage management with companies such as Dublin Grand Opera Society, New Zealand International Festival of the Arts and Wexford Festival Opera. Completed Motley Theatre Design Course in August 1995. Recent work includes assisting on **Fields of Ambrosia** (Aldwych) and costume designer on **Three Sisters** (Whittier Theatre, Los Angeles).

Charlotte Hall (Deputy Stage Manager)
Trained at Aberystwyth University. Theatre includes Stage Manager for **Cat and Mouse (Sheep)** and **Services** (Gate) and **Dracula** (Steam Industry at BAC), DSM **Silverface** (Gate) and ASM for **The Oginski Polonaise** and **Sisters, Brothers** (Gate). Publicity team member, National Student Theatre Company (Edinburgh '94) and Company Manager, National StudentTheatre Company (Edinburgh '95) .

Rose Keegan (Peterchen)
Trained at Central. Theatre includes Norma in Ayckbourn's **The Revenger's Comedies** (Strand), Linda in **A Message for the Broken Hearted** (Liverpool Playhouse and BAC), written by Gregory Motton and directed by Ramin Gray. Television includes **Miss Marple: The Mirror Cracked from Side to Side**, Mary Shelley in **The Story of Frankenstein** (YTV), **Under the Hammer** by John Mortimer (Carlton). Film includes **First Knight**.

Katrina Levon (Rosy)
Trained at Central School of Speech and Drama. Theatre includes **The Last Days of Don Juan, Love's Labour's Lost**, **Troilus and Cressida** and **Dr Jekyll and Mr Hyde** (RSC), **Outside of Heaven**, **Man of Mode** and **The Libertine** (Royal Court), **Manpower** (NT Studio), **The Impresario from Smyrna** (Old Red Lion), **Somewhere** and **Murmuring Judges** (NT).

Television includes **The Gospels**, **Ruth Rendell Mystery**, **Inspector Morse**, **Touch of Frost** and **Backup**. Film includes **Requiem Apache** and **Morris Motors**.

Rosa Maggiora (Designer)
Theatre includes **Venus and Adonis** and **Happy Days** (Glasgow Citizens Theatre), **How to Cook a Wolf** (BAC), **Party Girls** (Theatre Royal, Stratford East), **Easter** (RSC Pit), **Crocodile Looking at Birds**, co-designed with Rae Smith (Lyric Studio), **Voices on the Wind** (National Theatre Studio) and **Making the Future** (Oxford Stage Company – Young Vic).

Indhu Rubasingham (Director)
Trained at Hull University in Drama and was awarded an Arts Council Director's Bursary to work at Theatre Royal, Stratford East. Productions there include **Party Girls** by Debbie Plentie and the devised pieces **D'Yer Eat With Your Fingers?!** and **D'Yer Eat with Your Fingers – The Re-Mix**. Worked for Humphrey Barclay Productions developing a sit-com pilot for the BBC. Directed **Voices on the Wind** by Tanika Gupta (National Theatre Studio) and **A Doll's House** (Talawa Arts/Young Vic). Received the Karabé Award (1995) donated by Jenny Hall to work as Associate Director at The Gate.

Anthony Vivis (Translator)
Chair of the Translators' Association. Freelance translator for stage, radio and television since 1983, with translations appearing at the Royal Court, Traverse, Crucible and Leicester Haymarket theatres. He has specialized in translations of Fassbinder, Karge and Kroetz, and many new contemporary playwrights. In 1995 the Gate performed his and John Grillo's translation of Sperr's **Hunting Scenes from Lower Bavaria** and the Royal Court presented a reading of **Sugar Dollies**.

David Warwick (Stage Manager)
During the six years he has worked in theatre, his experience has covered most aspects of theatre production; from lighting for **Macbeth** and pantomimes, to making oversized props for **Godspell**, then having to sit in the band pit and throw up props to the actors on stage. Recently worked on productions of **Natural Causes** and **Time and Time Again** at the Victor Graham Comedy and Drama Season in Ayr and toured as stage manager with 2 TIE projects.

Sugar Dollies

Klaus Chatten
Translation by Anthony Vivis

Characters

Rosy
Babette Mrugalla
Tabea Mrugalla
Viola Pfauweber
Peterchen
Two **Policemen**

Setting: Present-day Germany.

Note
Rosy does not have an S problem.
The women's roles should be played by women. The parrot is male.

This text went to press before the opening night and may therefore differ from the version as performed.

For Anke Buff

Round One

Prologue without a theatre

Rosy *is sitting on a chair in front of the curtain. She is wearing a simple black dress and a faded jeans jacket. She is reading a script. She is around thirty and looks attractive.*
Beside her chair is a transparent audition case which is stuffed full of various articles she needs. She opens it from time to time to check the props.
She makes an effort to radiate total confidence in any given situation.
Around her neck hangs a closed pocket mirror.
Every so often she glances at the audience and nods encouragingly to people coming in.
She opens her pocket mirror and puts on some lipstick.
The lights go down.
A spot on **Rosy**.

Rosy (*calmly gets to her feet and clears her throat*)   I don't want to pull any wool over your eyes.
My name's Rosy.
I'm an actor and I've been out of work for two years.
I'll get started then.

She concentrates for a moment, then sings with the appropriate gestures in signed language 'I Will Survive'.

(*Enthusiastically to the audience.*) AND altogether.

Pause.

Briefly gives a signed rendition of 'Silent Night' then breaks off. Offended she picks up her props case and the chair. She is about to go off but then walks right upstage and stares at the audience.

(*Reproachfully.*) I grew up on a stripped-pine housing estate south-east of Hanover. Until I was sixteen I was forced to eat toasted liver sausage sandwiches and marrowbone soup with dumplings off tablecloths with swastikas embroidered on them.

Embroidered on BOTH SIDES, mind.
But you're not thinking that I turned
My back
On the economic miracle and my childhood concentration
camp
In order to get gold stars from overstressed directors of
studies for heavy academic classical sagas of ancient times
You're not thinking that
You're not THINKING that, are you?

*The props case bursts open of its own accord and out fall a large number
of paperbacks, a pitbull terrier mask, a Hitler moustache, a Russian
dictionary, a retractable sword, a length of rope, a helmet, several pairs
of glasses, some noses, banknotes, some cosmetics, snapped-off aerials
and Mercedes badges. She sticks the Hitler moustache on and stares
provocatively at the audience.*

Exactly a month ago the AGENCY forced me
Forced me
To accept a Job Creation job as a singing telegram.
I had to go to East Berlin dressed up as Hitler and sing 'My
Way' IN RUSSIAN at a youth initiation ceremony.

A long pause.

*Then in fantasy Russian she sings 'My Way' whilst signing 'I Will
Survive' and 'Silent Night'. She picks up the sword and hacks away at
the curtain in fury.*

Oh fuck fuck fuck fuck.

Gets on her knees, grabs an armful of scripts and buries her face in them.

Men we never meet write plays we act from eight to eleven at
night.
And the whole time all we can think of is our night off.

She goes on complaining and gives the pile of paperbacks a stir.

The only thing I've ever wanted is for the auditorium to
swing round like a revolve stage.
Swing round on its own axis.
So that the punters bow and the actors applaud.
Bloody stupid of course all bloody bloody stupid.

(*Thinking hard.*) But it's a nice idea and one that's always moved me.

Really moved me.

She comes across a paperback which she holds out at arm's length and immediately grows calmer.

(*Solemnly.*) Here, Tigris, come to me, I need you now.

She stands up again.

It all started with that audition for THE AGENCY.

I'd been working on *Penthesilea.* Here, Tigris, come to me, I need you now.

(*Laid back.*) The famous passage Here, Tigris, come to me, I need you now.

Where Penthesilea calls her dogs together to attack her lover Achilles and tear him limb from limb.

(*Uncompromising.*) No dogs of course NO scene.

So I asked my partner to get hold of a pitbull terrier outfit from a costume hiring firm.

(*Horrified.*) Whereupon the AGENCY wanted to take us on their books as a DOUBLE ACT Teeny Titch and Terrier Tom.

But I fought tooth and nail.

Tooth and nail.

And in the end

After a lot of grief and aggro

They put me down as a Juve Tear-jerker.

(*Proud and defiant.*) I play high octane emotionals.

That's what my Personality Profile came up with. Intensely Emotional Character.

PenthesileaMedeaJudithSalome.

If you'd just put yourselves in my shoes for a moment

I do Juliet as an audition piece and end up playing her like Stanley Kowalski.

With my emotional range the director EXPECTS me to do paternal feelings but all he GETS is a castration complex.

(*Hypnotised.*) And of course once implanted it STAYS.

A year ago in Memmingen against the express advice of my agent Frau von Dönitz I did do *Penthesilea* again.

Sure the Artistic Director's wife threw up but I still wasn't
hired.
There he stood in front of me that poor little man
With

She points out the vomit.

All down his herringbone sportsjacket.
My wife loved it he said. But we can't offer you a job. Because
you've got quite a serious S problem.
Do you know something I answered back If you take an
historical perspective this whole country has got a pretty
serious SS problem. So with my S problem I'm sure I'd just
about cope.
I've lost all faith in any POSITIVE FATHER-FIGURE.

She is about to go off.

I'm having therapy.
(*Emphatically.*) I'm having therapy because German Artistic
Directors (*Quoting.*) ALONG WITH their wives only have
to see ME to throw up and get a castration complex.
And anyway I'm not sure any more if it was the Artistic
Director who threw up and his wife who had a castration
complex or the other way about.
And in the final analysis who cares.
What interests ME personally a great deal more is this.
WHY doesn't anybody ask ME what I feel whenever I see
German directors ALONG WITH their wives?
WHY?

Pause.

(*Casually.*) And there we suddenly are in the heart of the
hurricane.
Do you know what happens when you lose your faith in a
POSITIVE FATHER-FIGURE?
(*Reproachfully.*) Do you know?

She picks up her case.

(*Pleasantly.*) Have a nice evening. (*Talking to an ASM off.*)
Curtain.

Rosy *goes off.*

The curtain opens.

Scene One

A bathroom with yellowish-white tiles and fringed rugs.
A loo.
A bidet.
A white door.
A bath.
And in the bath a clothes-drier with mohair women's underwear
hanging on it. A light-blue water-heater with its enamel peeling off. On
the loo sits **Tabea** *in a Robin costume, weeping. She is fat, wears*
glass-block spectacles and has an Ivanhoe haircut.
Stuck in her belt she has a large pair of scissors.
Around her neck hangs a leather money-bag and a scrap of violet
material.
Attached to her shoulder is a contraption which holds a mouth-organ.
Behind the door, invisible to the audience, lurks **Tabea**'s *mother*
Babette.

Babette   Tabea.
Tabea.
I'll beat you till you laugh if you don't watch it.

Tabea   Push off you fucking old witch of a mother.
Never again is our Tabea going to budge from here.
Never never never never never ever again.

Babette (*mock-friendly*)   Darling daughter, open the door
for Mummy please.
Mummy has to do wee-wees.

Pause.

Tabea for God's sake HURRY UP.

Tabea *sobs more violently.*

Babette   TABEA.
(*Extremely aggressive.*) I'll chuck you down the cellar.

Sounds of an axe chopping at the door. **Tabea** *screams, wrenches the loo-paper from its holder and begins to mummify herself with it.*

Babette   At the command – ONE.

She swings the axe.

At the command – TWO.

She swings the axe.

At the command – THREE.

She pokes her head through the hole.

Don't you imagine I'm going to pay for the damage. I'm taking it out your pocket money.

Tries but fails to reach the door key.

(*To herself.*) DON'T put off till the morrow what you can do today.

She goes on swinging the axe.

At the command – FOUR.

She goes on axing.

FIVE.
And

She goes on axing.

SIX.

With a body-check movement **Babette** *bursts into the bathroom. The door splinters.*

Babette *is wearing a Batman costume.*
The ears of her mask droop down long and limp.
She has stuck a wooden spoon into her yellow belt.
With legs apart and brandishing the axe **Babette** *stations herself in front of the bath.*
Tabea *pretends to be dead.*

Babette (*calmly*)   Right.
Let's talk to each other like two grown people, shall we? If you can hear me nod.

Tabea *nods*.

Babette   Now Mummy's going to ask you the sixty-four thousand-dollar question.
Are you a true professional or not?
(*Talking posh.*) THAT is the question we all want the answer to.

Tabea (*apologetically*)   I'm not a true professional.

Babette (*quietly threatening*)   YOU'RE not a true professional.

She sits down on the edge of the bath.

I'm going quietly spare.
Tabea performing for a solid hour will get the Carnival off to a good start.
I've been dinning the text into you since the middle of June.
Is it such a problem, then?
Listen, love, there's two versions.
TWO.
ONE tonight, that's the longer version, right. But the one tonight is just for fun. Tonight doesn't really matter, OK.
Tonight's just Shrove Tuesday Ladies' Night, all right.
But come Saturday . . .
It all starts getting serious. You perform the shorter version then, all right. And all the men will be there. THAT's the one that matters, Tabea. Saturday night.
CARNIVAL opening night.
Can't you get it into your thick head?
(*Insistently desperate.*) You've got to believe what you're saying. You talk like a fart in a high wind. What I'm saying is ONE cog has to engage with another. (*Gesturing.*) One ENGAGING WITH another.
(*Lovingly.*) Now when Mummy tells you something . . .

Conducting with her wooden spoon.

(*Tastelessly.*) IN my costume with its massive titty here I come to Gotham City. And I've got my Robin with me.
What does our little Tabea have to say for herself?

Pause.

Tabea *sobs again loudly and shakes her head in despair.*

Babette   What does our little Tabea have to say for herself?

Grabs her by the mouth-organ.

(*Very calmly.*) AND for you I'll play a ditty.
I've just about HAD enough, my girl.

She smashes the axe into the tiles then stuffs the mouth-organ into
Tabea's *mouth.*

If you think you can bugger everything up for me you've got
another think coming.

Unintelligible mouth-organ squeaks.

Tabea   Stop it Mum stop it stop it please you're hurting
me.

Babette   YOU try having your bosoms put through the
mangle THEN you'll know what pain is.
You made a total prat of me once before and that was once
too often.

Tabea (*bawling and tweeting*)   Come on, that wasn't my
fault.

Babette   Stop that bloody bleating, can't you?
If your father had been alive to see it, his own flesh and blood
tearing her maidenhead doing the splits at Carnival opening
night – God HELP us all.

Tabea (*she looks at her then bursts into tears*)   I want my dad.

Babette (*quietly*)   For Chrissake shut up.

She sits back down on the edge of the bath.

Let's not be too hard on ourselves, Tabea. Let's hope YOU
get another man. The way to your Wedding Night leads
either through LOADS of laughs or to a dead end.
Who do you think I'm putting the vermilion on for?

Tabea (*impassively*)   Oh, Dad. My dad.

Babette   My dad. My dad.
I'm just about SICK of hearing it.
You are twenty-six years old now.
Dad's been dead for twelve years. You can't still be blaming
Dad for your fat bum and your lousy memory after twelve
years.

Gives her a sceptical look.

Even as a child you were a bit peculiar.
How many times did I have to yank dead animals out your
doll's pram?
You'd picked them all up off the motorway.
Cats dogs birds rabbits.
And
Where were they lying?
Next to Pooh Bear and Cindy Doll.

Tabea *grins with satisfaction.*

Babette (*lowering her voice*)   YOU was never normal.

Sizing her up.

You're already much too old for your black friend from
America so you can forget him. If he ever decides to divorce
again HE'll marry his pet monkey rather than you. He'd get
more out of it.
Or do you feel like climbing up some palm tree at the (*She
tries to remember the name.*) Jackson Ranch and fetching him
DOWN a coconut.
That what you want?

Tabea (*defiantly*)   Nah, that's EXACTLY what I don't
want.

Babette   Well, at least you're honest, I'll give you that.
(*Sceptically.*) I do wonder sometimes. Your whole room full of
stuffed animals and that black man on your wall. Isn't it all a
bit funny?

Tabea (*proudly*)   AND the pin-up of Wim de Cuyp and his
Kalina de Sampinka IN her wedding dress.

Babette (*threateningly*)   Chrrrist if YOU only knew.

Tabea *is not listening.*

Tabea   MY dad. (*Opens her mouth in a vulgar way and retches.*)

Babette   Wish I had your imagination.

She takes a bottle out of the bathroom cabinet and drinks from it.

(*To herself.*) Klosterfrau Melissengeist. No BETTER way to revivify the over-fifties.

She cleans her teeth.

None of this is anywhere near a good subject for a successful evening, I can see that.

Takes off **Tabea**'s *glasses, spits on them and cleans them.*
Tabea *puts the mouth-organ to her lips and gives a soulful rendition of* 'The Green Green Grass of Home' *by Tom Jones.*

The mood changes.

Babette *looks at her lovingly, combs her hair, then glances at her wrist-watch, takes a phial from the bathroom cabinet and dabs some perfume behind her Batman ears.*

(*Dreamily.*) Rapture by Yardley for that special man.
Right.
Now you be nice to your mum again please.

Tabea (*unwraps all the loo-paper from her head and nods*)   Yep. I always am anyway, Mum.

They hug.

Babette (*produces an envelope from her sleeve, kisses it, then puts it back. She sings*)   If you knew.
If YOU only knew.

Turns completely around and hums the signature tune of a television programme.

IF YOU only knew.

Tabea (*snatches at the envelope*)   Hurry up, open that thing and quick about it.

Babette *takes up position on the edge of the bath brandishing her wooden spoon.*

Babette (*uncompromising*)   No.
First carry on sewing your mum's costume.

Tabea (*brusquely*)   Yep.

Gets up from the loo pulls up her flesh-coloured tights and Robin shorts and hums vivaciously.

Can you remember?
Can you remember when Dad mixed up his schnapps and the fruit juice for our kids' punch and all us little brats nearly died FROM alcohol poisoning?
HOW old was I then?

Babette *is still trying to think.*

Babette (*casually*)   Eight innocent years old, my little angel.

Tabea   What kind of costume did I used to wear at that age?

Babette   You went as a member of the Ku Klux Klan.

Tabea   What?

Babette   You went as a member of the Ku Klux Klan.
And you won First Prize out the whole hall. As sure as my name's Babette Mrugalla. The First Prize.

Sings Gary Glitter's 'You want to be in MY Gang'.

In those days Gary Glitter was the beefcake pin-up on your nursery wall.
(*She tries to remember.*) I'd just brought in a plate of cold cuts into the living-room And there you were stretched flat out ba-boom.
You and all the other little brats from the area.
Like loads of brightly coloured ants.
All OVER my Berber carpet.
(*To herself.*) Suffer the little children to come unto me.
I suffered all you pirates, princesses and little devils.
FIRST I had to put my finger (*Michelangelo's painting of God's finger touching Adam.*)
DOWN your throat to stop you choking, then siren blowing

blue light flashing all the way to St Mary's Hospital
(*Pompously*.) And your innocent young life was hanging by a
scalpel edge.
And your mum was back in the shit again because of that old
piss artist.

A long pause.

Tabea (*with a piercing stare*)   Mum.

Pause.

Mum, if you kill the mate of a black mamba
The other mate will follow your tracks for twenty-four hours
At breakneck speed
There's no fighting it – SO fast –
Till it catches up with you.

A long pause.

Babette *has not noticed the change of mood.*

Babette (*casually*)   Where on earth do YOU pick up such
information?

With some balletic mouth movements she tries to memorise her text.

Tabea   FROM my boss.

Picks up her leather money-bag.

Fairground bonbons.
There is NOTHING to touch them.

Babette *reaches out.*
Tabea *reluctantly gives her a bonbon.*

Tabea (*warning her*)   With A SINGLE blow of my rapier I
can split your skull.

Babette (*goes on axing*)   YOU shouldn't keep saying things
like that to your poor old mum.

Tabea (*overlapping*)   I'm an animal keeper. You can't
afford to be too soft.
(*Defiantly to herself.*) BORNEO we brought back some
cannibal cutlery from there.
Do you know what the local people there call white people?

Pause.

(*Piercingly.*) Mum.

Babette (*still memorising her text loudly*)   SILVER-arrow.

Tabea (*screeching*)   You're SO thick.
You're SO thick.
(*Teasing.*) Silver-arrow, you thicko, Silver-arrow, you
thicko.
(*Brusquely.*) Right then.
For that I'm demoting you to Private.
The people of Borneo call white people long-pigs.
(*Pointing to* **Babette**.) For all YOUR anti-baby pills loads of
animals have had to suffer.
A HUNDRED THOUSAND rats
Cut open and for weeks on end sewn together again while still
conscious.
Oh yes.
It's a tough world in business.
(*Kitschily.*) The loveliest experience.
The loveliest experience WE ever had. In South Africa we
cut ourselves on a knife. In the zoo in Johannesburg. There
we were standing outside the cage with rhesus monkeys in it.
And one of the baby rhesus monkeys licked our wounds. And
our arms.

Does the same on **Babette**.

Like this.
Like this.
Round and round us.
Round and round and back again.

Babette *almost falls into the bath.*

Tabea   ROUND AND ROUND the cage.
And wept BUCKETS the poor little monkey did. Buckets.
(*Proudly.*) That was MY experience.

Babette   You tell lies whenever YOU open your mouth.
YOU've NEVER been to Johannesburg.

Tabea (*casually*)   OK, but my boss has.

Stops short.

I haven't got enough material.

Babette   I'm quite happy with what I got.

She looks at herself in the mirror and pulls her ears up again.

Lick my arse, Mum, looks really smashing, don't you think?

Tabea   YOU and your fat bum.

Babette   The effects of the menopause that is, you've got all that to come.

Pause.

Right then, Tabea, my little treasure.
You go and sit down on our lovely bidet and hold on tight.

Tabea *does so.*

Babette (*takes out the letter*)   In THIS envelope Mum's got a little surprise.

Tabea (*screeching*)   But I don't want to go anywhere any more.

Babette   Calm down, love. You will want to go HERE. Mum sent off an application for her FAVOURITE daughter. You got three guesses. Starting now.

Tabea (*screeching*)   I don't want to leave my boss. I don't want to.

Babette   Don't worry, you don't have to leave HIM.

She holds on to the envelope and entices **Tabea**.

Come on then come on come on come on.

Tabea (*gets up and tries to snatch it*)   Come on, hand it over right now. That thing there. And quick about it.

Babette   Come on then come on come on come on.

Tabea *has almost got it.*

Babette (*pulls it away*)   Bad luck, you thicko. (*She laughs.*)

Tabea *loses her footing, brushes up against the bidet tap and squirts water all over herself.*
Babette *gets a fit of the giggles.*
Tabea *still screeching dries herself off with a hand-towel.*
Babette *wrenches the towel from her hands and chucks it away.*

Babette (*threateningly*)   WHAT is Tabea's favourite programme?

Tabea (*screeching*)   *Wildlife on . . .*

Babette (*furiously*)   What?

Tabea (*screeching*)   WHEN the curtain goes up on Wim de Cuyp and Kalina de Sampinka.

Babette   Yehhss.

Pulls out her wooden spoon.

(*Demanding.*) AND?
And what else?

Tabea (*as if she knew it by heart*)   I face that man for the first time. That special man who is good enough for me.

Babette (*contentedly and crisply*)   Right.
(*Building up tension. One syllable at a time.*) In THIS envelope you'll find an invitation to Wim de Cuyp's blind date show. Addressed to

She tears the envelope open and reads out.

(*In astonishment.*) Our Tabea.

Silence.

Tabea *gasps for air then shrieks with delight.*
She goes down on her knees shuffles over to her mother and smothers her Batman rubber boots with kisses.

Tabea   Oh Mum, my darling darling Mum.
I can't POSSIBLY thank you enough as long as I live.
I simply can't.
Never ever ever ever.

Babette (*talking posh*)   You don't HAVE TO thank your mummy. She loves giving you things.

She sets **Tabea** *down on the bidet again.*

(*Casually*.) There's only one teeny weeny little snagline.

Tabea's *heart misses a beat.*

Babette (*brightly*)   I SENT them your cousin's photo.

Horrified pause.

Yes, well, Tabea.
You and that Lydia used to be as alike as two peas.
But now Now YOU don't need Lydia ANY more for
nothing. You're in a class of your own.

She again indicates colossal plumpness.

Tabea   Right and what now?

Babette (*casually*)   LOSE some weight
Till you're good enough for your mystery sweetheart.

Tabea *stares hard at* **Babette**, *opens her money-bag, throws the
fairground bonbons down the loo and flushes them away.*

Babette (*addressing the audience in a posh voice*)   Any other
response from my daughter would have DEEPLY
disappointed me.

They embrace and remain with their arms around one another.

(*She whispers rapidly*.) We've got THREE months my angel
I've looked out a load of diets for you. (*Jovially*.) And Mum
will join in.
We've already plumped for pineapples. Nothing but fresh
healthy fruit from the jungle.
NOTHING BUT healthy food.
NOTHING BUT abstinence.

She releases **Tabea** *and has a good look at her.*

(*Demanding*.) But right now I've got another little problem
here.

She looks at her watch and briefly raises her wooden spoon.

Tabea *stands there bolt upright and looks out into the audience.*

Babette   In my costume with its massive titty here I come
to Gotham City and I've got my Robin with me

Tabea   And for you I'll play a ditty.

Babette   If you're feeling bruised and bad

Tabea   We'll make sure you don't stay sad.

Babette (*sits down on the edge of the bath and shakes her
head*)   Need nerves of reinforced steel to cope with you.
(*In a posh voice.*) EVERYTHING'S ALL RIGHT AGAIN
NOW.

Tabea *pulls a face and gruffly points to* **Babette** *and the bath.*

Tabea (*concentrating hard*)   A human being only has to lie in
icy water for four minutes and they're STONE dead.
HEART attack.

Pause.

Babette (*looks daggers at* **Tabea**)   Just do me one small
favour.
WHEN you're on Wim de Cuyp's blind date show, *Sugar
Dollies*, steer clear of these subjects please.

Tabea   What else am I supposed to talk about, then?

Babette (*thinks for a moment*)   You are skating on thin ice,
girl.

A long silence.

I always knew
YOU killed Dad
And now
You've just given the game away.

Tabea *sits down heavily and defiantly on the loo and takes off her
glasses.*

Babette (*piecing the accusation together sentence by sentence*)
YOU knew he always used to hide his schnapps in the water-
butt.
Every night he'd disappear out my double bed, down the
garden.

(*Horrified.*) Suddenly it's all falling into place like a jigsaw
puzzle.
You waited for EXACTLY THE RIGHT night.
Icy cold.
Below zero.
And getting colder.
YOU had hidden the schnapps.
He was looking for it
FOR SEVERAL MINUTES in his water-butt.
He looked and looked, that poor husband of mine.
After FOUR minutes a heart attack.
(*Piecing the rest together*.) Overnight frost.
And him
(*She starts to cry.*) FROZEN SOLID in the water-butt. That's
how it was.
It's all clear to me now, Tabea.
And his bottle of schnapps.
Never came to light and
And MY daughter is the murderess. Fuck and bugger it.
(*Emphasising each syllable.*) How could YOU do that to me?
I've always been a good mum to you.
Where did I go wrong?

Tabea *pulls a bottle of schnapps out from behind the loo.*

Tabea (*in a posh voice*)   My darling mother, I ALWAYS
have this bottle WITHIN reach.

Babette (*goes on crying*)   AND my God the way you CRIED
on my breast.
And the firemen helping
To thaw Dad out with a blowlamp.

Pulling off some loo-paper, she blows her nose.

YOU belong in prison, you murderer.
(*Shrieking.*) You MURDERER.
MURDERER.
MURDERER.
For THIS you'll have to pay all your life, you filthy bitch.
YOU'RE a criminal.
YOU didn't just kill.

YOU killed your own father.
YOU committed the worst crime a human being can
possibly imagine
IN this lovely world of ours.

She spits in **Tabea**'s *face, then crosses herself.*

(*Hypnotised.*) For this you'll roast in hell FOR all eternity,
you filthy bitch.

Tabea   But THIS TIME NOT alone.

She spits in her face.

Babette *crosses herself, stands up, takes a cigarette out of her pocket
and lights it. Then she pulls her axe out of the tiles, goes out, shuts the
door and sticks her head through the hole.*

Babette   Murderer.

Tabea (*letting her delight show through her clenched teeth she
sings*)   Schnapps.
That's the last thing he had to say before the angels carried
him away, (twice).

*She looks for more fairground bonbons in her money-bag, tips it out,
then gives up.*

(*Tonelessly.*) Fe Fi Fo Fum. Spray some water on your bum.

She sits down on the bidet tap and water spurts out.

Blackout.

Scene Two

A small temporary conference room in an East Berlin hotel.
Antiseptic post-modern furnishings.
A window with plastic blinds and curtains.
On the wall a large Baroque oil-painting.
*A door marked EXIT which is padded on the inside and which leads
into the function room.*
In the corner a parrot's cage.
A writing-desk.

*Behind the desk an armchair. Draped over the armchair a lightweight
fashionable national costume jacket.
Beside this a tea-trolley.
On the tea-trolley a tray with a silver dish-cover.
In front of the desk a swivel armchair on which a video camera is
trained.
On the desk a colour television set showing a freeze-frame picture of the
empty swivel chair.
Non-alcoholic refreshments.
A champagne-cooler.
Tea and coffee.
A basket of biscuits.
A pile of forms.
A ceiling-fan on the ceiling.*

Viola, *a woman of around thirty-five, is sitting on the window-seat.
She is dressed in a sportily conservative style and blows air on to her face
from a small hand-fan. She is talking into a cordless telephone.*

In the swivel chair sits **Peterchen**, *a woman of the same age. She is
brown from the sun, is wearing a fringed leather jacket and has her
hand deep in her sequined handbag.*

Peterchen *looks for an ashtray, but in the end flicks her ash into the
lid of her cigarette box.*

The ceiling-fan stops.

Viola   Nonononono he DIDN'T burp. Nonononono I was
listening very carefully. And I distinctly heard (*Matter of
fact.*) Saab yes Saab (*Enticingly in baby-talk.*) Eeyess. (*Pause.*)
Eeyess. (*Pause.*) Eeyess. (*Pause.*) What did my sweetie say to
Mummy then? (*Pause.*) WHAT did my sweetie say to
Mummy? What a clever boy. (*Matter of fact.*) Saab.

Peterchen *looks at her with dismay.*

Viola (*sings*)   You sing too then. Daddy doesn't believe
Mummy. You sing too. (*Pause.*) WHAT did my sweetie say
to Mummy?
Don't force him, darling. Don't.
I AM not disappointed. What rubbish. (*She groans wearily.*)
(*Edgily.*) Oh my God. THE heat. A First-Class Hotel with no

air-conditioning. Unbelievable. And the fan gives up the
ghost after ten minutes. But all is not lost. I have a red parrot
here in my room. East is East and West is West and never the
twain shall gel.
Rejects from Cuba I expect.
Not bad actually. Not bad at all. Seventh floor. Very central
location. (*Opening the blinds. Some way off we see the nearby
Reichstag.*) Stick your thumb down his throat. (*Following
straight on.*) But if the city wants to be internationally
competitive again there'll need to be quite a few changes
made I can tell you. QUITE A FEW.
(*To* **Peterchen**.) Can YOU read notices by any chance?

Peterchen   Yes.

Viola *points to a No Smoking sign on the wall.*
Peterchen *looks around and she is so upset she stubs the cigarette out
in her own palm.*

Peterchen (*very nervous*)   Oh God, sorry, I'm afraid I
didn't.

Viola (*has already stopped listening to her*)   And me very very
very much.
(*Brusquely.*) Oh God, people here just don't have faces.
(*Covers the mouthpiece.*) You were saying.

Peterchen   It was him over there.

The **Parrot** *makes sucking noises.*

Parrot (*questioning*)   Kiss kiss. Gissa kiss then. (*Whining.*)
Hiyaaahhh.

Makes sucking noises.

(*Questioning.*) Kiss kiss. (*In a piercing voice.*) Hiyaaahhh.

Viola *picks up her national costume jacket and throws it over the cage.
The* **Parrot** *jabbers furiously and is then silent.* **Viola** *drops her
hand-fan which shatters.*
Viola *looks daggers at* **Perterchen**.
Peterchen *jumps up and collects the fragments.*

Peterchen   Rummage rummage. Search search.

Lays the bits on the desk.

Viola (*turns away*)   I AM sorry, I really am.
(*Interrupting*.) My meal is getting cold, right.
And give my Sweetie a big kiss and cuddle.
Bye, bye-bye.

She switches off and groans. Sits in her armchair, reaches into the champagne-cooler, takes out some ice-cubes and puts them in her armpits to cool herself down.

Just a minute.

Takes off the dish-cover and starts to eat.

Peterchen   Bon appétit.

Viola *nods and eats.*

Pause.

Peterchen *stares at her plate.*

Peterchen   Not just pearl onions and braid-sausages.

Viola (*pointing to her basket*)   Cheese roll.

Peterchen   No thanks.

Pause.

But the potato cornets look very tasty.

Viola *looks up sceptically.*

Peterchen   Cro

Viola (*with her mouth full*)   quettes.
(*As if to a foreigner*.) They're known as croquettes.

Peterchen   Croquettes.

Pause.

The Hotel Lindenkorso before the Wall came down served the best potato cornets in the world.

Viola (*groans*)   OK, fine, you know best.

She uses the remote control to switch the video camera on. **Peterchen**
appears on the screen. **Viola** *turns the TV set towards her, picks up a
form and goes on eating.*

You're from the former Eastern Zone I take it.

Peterchen   That's right.

Viola   Right.

Pause.

Peterchen   We didn't know what was going on.

Viola   Come again.

Peterchen (*shakes her head*)   Nothing.

Viola (*reading*)   PETER.
First name.

Peterchen (*cutting in*)   CHEN PeterCHEN.
The first name's so long I'm not sure even my mother knew it
all.

Viola *gives a short laugh.*
*Without warning she claps her hands, then spreads them out in best
chat-show-host fashion and suddenly becomes very friendly.*
Peterchen *shudders in shock.*

Viola   Let's have a nice relaxing chat together, shall we?
Now why don't you tell me a bit about yourself?

Peterchen   Right. Well, I . . . (*Pause.*) In the former GDR
for ten years I was mostly working in ash disposal. Since the
Wall came down –

Viola   Sorry, in –

Peterchen (*without thinking*)   In the medical corps. Of the
National People's Army. Since the Wall came down I've
been working as a Girl Friday.
In a sunshine-studio.

Viola   So in your new career
You're better off than before.

Peterchen   It beats washing out soldiers' foot-cloths.

Viola   Now this sunshine-studio.
Is it in the West or the East?

Peterchen (*clearing her throat*)   If it's OK to say this here

Leaning forward towards the camera.

WE are the Happy Sunshine Brigade.
Where we live in the East the sun NEVER SETS. Us
troopers in the Happy Sunshine Brigade enjoy round-the-
clock HIGH SPIRITS. We're always on Red Alert.

Viola (*puts her knife and fork down*)   Shall we try to get one
thing clear from the outset? The sort of people we're looking
for are whizzy fizzy types.
People who are frustrated
People
With problems
Which stick out like sore thumbs
Are not for us.
Is that clear?

Peterchen (*quickly*)   Yes yes absolutely clear.

Pause.

If I could just interrupt A MOMENT. Umm, where are the
two –

Viola   Two what?

Peterchen   Kalina de Sampinka and Wim de Cuyp.

Viola (*reeling it off as she has a thousand times before*)   Look,
what you and I are here to do is (*Parenthetically.*) a spot of, if
you like, casting.

Peterchen   Yes, it said that on the invitation. What is it
exactly?

Viola *groans*.

Viola (*waving an identity card in her face*)   My name's Viola
Pfauweber and I'm from SUGAR DOLLIES.
My job and the job of the men and women I work with is to

suggest guests to appear on the television show hosted by these two very popular stars.

Peterchen   Ah, right with YOU now, a broadcast.

Viola (*calmly*)   Selecting suitable guests for a broadcast or rather transmission.

Peterchen   Suggest a guest for a broad host, right? And there I was thinking –

Viola   Thinking is best left to horses.

She goes on eating.

Peterchen (*is about to take hold of a cigarette but then rubs her palms*)   Do you think that parrot's getting enough air?

Viola *gives her another withering look.*

Peterchen   Not that it's any of my business.

Viola   Correct.

She reads.

(*Smugly.*) SPACE RESEARCH in the (*In quotation marks.*) former GDR.
Inter-galactic Trabbies.
I must say you people had more sense of humour than we realised.
It says something about a watch here.

Peterchen   A cosmonaut's watch.

She leans forward to camera again.

When I was still in the Pioneers, I'd seen one in the SUBHA newspaper.
I even offered to swap my guinea-pig for it.
And a couple of days later the SUBHA reporters were knocking at my door.

Viola (*asking a question*)   SUBHA?

Peterchen (*without thinking*)   Sing up and be happy.
(*As if talking to a foreigner.*) SUBHA.
The reporters took thirty photos. Click click click. And one

week later –
Right, hand over your guinea-pig.
Ogh, I said he's a bit peeky right now and he's over the hill,
but I've got this album with some Soviet Solidarity stamps
inside.
You can have all that.

Viola *laughs*.

Peterchen   High Spirits round the clock.

Viola *switches the video camera off and leans back*.

Viola (*warmly*)   Tell me something, Peterchen.
There's one thing I personally don't understand IF you are
such a right-on sort of woman, how come you're still single,
hmm?

Peterchen (*thinks very hard*)   Well.
I don't quite KNOW either.
My two longest relationships lasted six months.

Takes out her wallet and shows her two photographs.

My men.
Torsten will be five next month and Ricardo Ricardo is
thirteen.

She looks at them herself.

Viola   Could you imagine relating to younger men,
Peterchen?

Peterchen (*without thinking*)   On principle I only have
relationships with twenty-four-year-old men.

Viola (*shocked*)   You have WHAT?

Peterchen   It's true.

Pause.

Viola (*concerned*)   Won't it be really destructive for you if
they show up one day with a twenty-year-old girlfriend?

Peterchen   Ogh, you know.
(*Thinking it through*.) My view is this If a bloke's going to leave
you it doesn't make any difference whether he's twenty-four

or sixty. If THAT's what worries you you can always do without.

(*Jovially.*) Only yesterday I was telling Ricardo, your new percussion teacher is someone I could really go for.

She winks at **Viola**.
Viola *leans back aghast.*

Pause.

She claps her hands together, closing the subject.

Viola (*in a matey way*)   Right.
Now what will you wear if you join our team?

Peterchen   My old camouflage outfit.

Viola   Come again.

Peterchen   Only joking, sorry.

She clears her throat.

If it's all right with you I'd like to come in my strapless dress.
And I'd have my hair up a bit like this.

Viola (*very friendly*)   Splendid.
You'll be hearing from us.
And now we just need your signature here and that's it for now.

Peterchen (*signs*)   What have I signed?

Viola (*puts the form away and holds out her hand*)   Just something for our peace of mind.

Peterchen *stays sitting there.*

Viola   Anything else I can do for you?

Peterchen   So I'll be hearing from you, then?

Viola   Uh-huh.

She points to the exit.
Peterchen *stands up and looks to camera.*

Peterchen   Right.
Well, I enjoyed that more than I thought I was going to.

Viola   Good.

Silence.

Peterchen (*quietly*)   I blew it, right.

Pause.

I'm a failure.

Viola   We don't talk in terms of FAILURE.

Pause.

Now you just sit yourself down again, love.

Peterchen *sits down.*

Viola   What I'm about to do NOW is strictly personal,
right. And I'm only doing it because I like you. Just keep it to
yourself, OK, I've a family to think of. Have we understood
each other?

Peterchen (*hoarse*)   Right, yeah.

Viola   I've been looking at you from every viewpoint.
Every conceivable viewpoint.
See for yourself, feel free.

She swivels the TV set complete with its freeze-frame picture towards
Peterchen.

Peterchen.
We don't often come across someone like you
But your viewability rating
Is next to NIL. In fact it's heading for a minus figure.

Pause.

As sorry as I am to say it, no way, José.
At this moment in time we just don't think the public are
ready for you. We'd be betraying the viewers' trust *vis-à-vis*
not just you but the whole political spectrum.
What we're here for is to make people feel good. Are you with
me? Feel good about life.
Us media folk have a mission, right?
Those of us who work in the entertainment area have a

specific POLITICAL job to do, OK. And that job is ...
Well, you tell me.

Peterchen   I'm er not quite sure I –

Viola (*insistent but concerned*)   YES.
YES YES YES AND YES AGAIN.
(*With real commitment.*) In spite of everything
YES in spite of everything in this ghastly awful terrible world
of ours
Let's show people its beauty. What's worth living for. And
loving for.
YES YES YES AND YES AGAIN.
I do realise THIS is a really really bad time for you. But even
if I reject you professionally one hundred per cent, on a
personal level, Peterchen, I like you a lot. Personally I'm
totally with you.
Look, there's simply no point in our giving you false hopes.
Six years after the currency union
It's about time you people started looking facts in the face.
(*Insistently.*) All the facts
Communism hasn't just wiped you out economically but it's
also totally destroyed your *joie de vivre* and your moral
capital.
You Easties are so set in concrete so unspontaneous so
unfeeling so totally trapped in habit. It's as if there's a lid
permanently screwed down on you. The lid of the
Communist Manifesto or WHATEVER.
But all I can do is shout hi there hi there hi there. Hi there all
you lovely brothers and sisters. Wakey wakey, that's all I can
shout.
Rise and shine, Peterchen. Enjoy your stay on earth.
But in your case RISE AND SHINE doesn't INCLUDE
brown-nosing to us quite so blatantly.
You've got to stand on your own two feet.
You've got to start from where you actually are now. Not
from ten paces further on.
That just isn't realistic.
(*Warmly.*) You pretended you were all sweetness and light
but in fact you ARE in a really lousy mood.

Peterchen   Right.

Viola (*hard*)   So why on earth try to be on an
ENTERTAINMENT show?
Let's start working together right now.
Let's draw up a balance sheet, OK.
Here and now.

She takes another look at the documents.

First point. You have regular sun-ray treatment.

Peterchen   I do, yes.

Viola   TOO MUCH.
Too much. Too much. Too much. I have sun-ray treatment
too.

Peterchen   You do?

Viola   But you'd never know it, right. And that's the point.
(*Insistently.*) You'd never know. One really crucial aspect of
interhuman contact is doing things in moderation, OK.
MODERATION.
As I said you're all too consumerist. Too greedy. Too
impatient. Too grasping.
And, oh my God, your arms. That's my Second Point. You
might just as well hack them off. You wouldn't even notice.
They're like so much larchlap fencing. So lifeless.
Do much sport, do you?

Peterchen   Yoga.

Viola (*overlapping*)   That's totally wrong for you. You need
to do something about your inhibitions. Take up a team
sport of some sort.
(*She takes a deep breath.*) AND Third Point. Bad bad bad really
bad. Sorry to be so heavy about it.
But your beer-bottle-boobs.

Peterchen (*overlapping*)   Beer-bottle-boobs.

Viola   Do you think everything on me is real?
Peterchen, I'm a woman with expensive tastes.

Pause.

We can talk so openly together. And that's great, isn't it? For
you Easties of course talking like this takes you only to point
zero, right.

Rummages in her files.

But to be honest with you it isn't only the former GDR that's
giving us hassle.
Here, for instance. The wrong attitude screams out at you
even from a Polaroid photo. (*Reading.*) Take Tabea
Mrugalla.
What our headhunter had in mind defeats me.
(*Asking herself a question.*) Category Two.

She puts that file to one side and picks up the next.

WHAT the hell.
We'll have to bin the lot.

She tosses that file into the waste-paper bin and picks up the next.

No students, I said.
We want people who have their feet on the ground.

She goes on searching.

But no two-point-fours either please. What we need. What
we need is somebody who's dangerous but still one of us.
Here we are, just the job. Some character into leather and
gynaecology. Calls himself THE HOLE-EXPLORER.
Now THAT's entertainment.

She picks up the next file.

Body-builders go down really well. But body-builders don't
grow on trees. Most body-builders aren't single any more
because they've got such great bodies.
As for this one . . .
He took the bleeding biscuit today.
A butcher with a wispy beard and crisply ironed shirt who
puts down his dog as his hobby and stinks to high heaven.
Unbelievable.
Real-life satire round the clock.
Why do people like that want to appear ON television?

They ought to be just watching TV or crawling down to the cellar.

Peterchen   In the Underground once I was sitting next to this dosser and he stank so much I had to move to another compartment. Sometimes you know what your parents mean when they say
THAT SORT OF THING NEVER HAPPENED IN HITLER'S DAY.

Silence.

Viola (*bends forward and talks very softly*)   You listen to me, Peterchen, and listen hard.

Peterchen   Right.

Viola   Sixty per cent of my husband's business partners are from abroad. FROM Switzerland, FROM America, FROM Israel, France, Great Britain.
They ring us up. They wake us up at night with their calls because on their tellies they're seeing window-panes smashed and houses on fire all over again. And what they're seeing I'm sorry to say ISN'T old newsreel footage. It's all on today's News. And they ask my darling and me
WHAT is going on in your country?
Have you still not worked it out?
Have you still not worked out how to keep these anti-social elements in check?
What kind of an impression do you lot think you're making on our trading partners?
Well, what's your honest opinion?

Pause.

Feel free.
You're only cutting your own throats after all.

Pause.

(*Indignant.*) My husband was telling me about a woman social worker from (*Reproachfully.*) Dresden who tried to rehabilitate a bunch of Neo-Nazis by taking them on holiday to Israel.

(*Unmistakably disgusted.*) To cure them of their anti-Semitism over there.

In other words YOU LOT in the former GDR are spending our taxes on bermuda shorts and suntan lotion for Saxon skinheads.

And in all probability that woman social worker of yours is on the beach at Tel Aviv right now rubbing sun-cream on thugs with SIEG HEIL tattooed all over them.

If I were to describe my fantasies when I think about that woman I'd end up in prison.

Peterchen   I think you've misunderstood what I was trying to say.

Viola   And it all started off so well.
WE ARE THE PEOPLE WE ARE THE PEOPLE.
Leipzig.
But what's left of all that now?
The Wall came down when my darling and I were on holiday, I'm afraid.
But one year later on October third we were stood right here on the spot.
My God, we were proud of you lot.
GERMANY IS GETTING MARRIED THE BRANDENBURG GATE IS HER ALTAR.
OK, fine, a yucky headline, granted.
(*Asking a question.*) But from the marketing angle quite a coup?
Hit the spot, eh?

Looking right at her.

Bugger all. Bugger all.
The Germans have understood BUGGER ALL.

Peterchen (*scarcely audible*)   On November ninth I was the only German from the Eastern sector to walk through the Brandenburg Gate.

Viola *leans back.*

Viola (*cynically*)   And how am I meant to take that?

Peterchen (*hesitating*)   On November ninth Ricardo
Torsten's father and me were on UNTER DEN LINDEN.
And the Platz der Republik was still sealed off by GDR
policemen THAT night.
(*Cautiously with a glance at* **Viola**.) The Pariser Platz.
Then we walked on till we reached the police barrier.
And all of a sudden I was standing by this fifty-year-old
policeman.
And I suddenly felt so angry and I started to scream and
scream.
(*In a very clear voice to* **Viola**.) Tonight I'M GOING to go
through that Gate.
Without non-existent great-aunts or non-existent great-
grandmothers to visit in the West.
Twenty-eight years I've been waiting for this and you
You are not going to stop me.
And Ricardo burst into tears and my ex-boyfriend tried to
calm me down.
But I felt the same as I did about that cosmonaut's watch
(*To* **Viola**.) You've got to stop all this, I shouted.
Stop it, you've got to stop it.
Or nothing whatsoever will ever really change.

Pause.

And the policeman didn't bat an eyelid.
And I was so frightened but I'd had it up to here.
Up to here I'd had it.
On the other side of the barrier some West Berliners were just
standing there. They'd jumped over the Wall from
SIEBZEHNTER JUNI Street.

At this moment the national costume jacket slips down from the
Parrot's *cage.*

Viola *and* **Peterchen** *briefly glance in that direction.*

Parrot (*whining*)   Hiya.

Viola   Go on.

She very carefully trains the camera on **Peterchen** *again and*
switches it on.

Peterchen   They were soaking wet from the water-
cannon.

Pause.

(*To* **Viola** *in a clear voice.*) YOU LOT stuck me in the army.
But you still didn't succeed in breaking me.
And tonight.
Yes tonight I am going to walk through that Gate. With my
head held high. And if you shoot me . . .
Then this young woman on the other side said to me: Take it
easy now
You just come through to us. Nobody's going to hurt you.

Pause.

(*Perplexed.*) And all the policemen stood to one side. Except
the one I'd shouted at.
And I climbed over the barrier and Ricardo was clinging to
me for dear life. But I had to do it. I just had to.
It was like that cosmonaut's watch for me.
(*Trying to remember.*) And with the young woman
There was a lad
With green hair
And the two of them walked either side of us.

Pause.

(*Emphatically.*) And then we walked on towards the Gate.

She tries to pull herself together.

TWENTY-EIGHT years. Oh my God, TWENTY-EIGHT
years.

Pause.

And once we
Were through that ghastly Gate
In front of me, in front of us on the Wall stood hundreds of
West Berliners.
And the policemen tried to shoot them off with water-
cannon.
But as we got nearer
Behind us

(*In surprise.*) All at once
Without looking round
And without warning
They suddenly
Lowered their water-cannon.
The Square was
So very still
(*In a considered and matter-of-fact way.*) Just as if the Bomb was
about to go off any minute.
And the people
On the Wall
Lifted up their hands
Like in a slow-motion film.

She stands up very slowly, makes a victory sign and in the process knocks the video camera over.

Like that.

Viola   And then
What happened next?

Peterchen   Then everybody howled yelled laughed cried.
The people on the Wall, the policemen, the young woman,
little Ricardo and me.
It was as if some vortex, some invisible vortex, was blowing
across the square and blowing it away.
Blowing it away to the end of the universe.
Far out beyond Orion.
As far as the ring nebula of Monoceros.
Then hurling it back from millions of light years away.
Then just as suddenly it was the same square again.
Simply there.

Pause.

Do you understand me? I'm no Nazi.
I'm not. I'm really not.
I only want to live my life.

Viola   Yes, I understand you very well.

Peterchen   Then we walked back to the barrier and the
policemen moved aside again.
Just like that.
Except for one of course.
And a young one at that.
A policeman.
He was all of eighteen.
He grabbed me by the sleeve, looked straight at me and said

Pause.

(*To* **Viola** *in a very matter-of-fact voice.*) Thank you so much.

She starts to cry.

And Ricardo's snot ran all down my shoulders.
AND my overcoat.
It just went on and on running.
And I so wanted to thank the two young people, the young
woman and the lad.
But suddenly they had gone.
(*Pulling herself together again.*) And then
Then we walked to the Invalidenstrasse transit point
On the Kurfürstendamm.
I rang my mother from Zoo Station.
All the West Berliners who walked past us dropped coins into
the telephones.
Because of course we had only notes.
Total strangers hugged each other.

Pause.

(*Thinking hard.*) Next morning when we wanted to go back
home my ex-boyfriend stayed in the West. Till the first shops
opened.
What he said was: The only things that'll interest me for the
next few years are porno films and fruit from the South.

Silence.

Viola   My God. You'll have me in tears any minute.
It's a really amazing story.
We can do something with this I'm sure.

It makes my creative juices run.
(*Thinking aloud.*) We'll have to put an ad in the paper. And
run those policemen to earth.
All of you get together in the studio. Not on OUR show
obviously.
YOU tell the story
Like you just have
Exactly that way.
We won't change A SYLLABLE.
Then the policeman gives us his side.
(*Thinking hard.*) And
(*Leans back.*) We'll have to show a balanced view of course. Be
fair to both parties. Obviously.
And needless to say you're the heroine of the midnight hour.
But I don't expect the bloke had it easy either.
I mean...
I mean, I bet he so wanted to walk through that Gate WITH
you.
But he was there officially.
He was there serving the state.
Serving a really really evil criminal regime.
And of course there's no excuse whatsoever.
But not everyone's born to be heroic. Like you.
I mean,
That man and his family
Feared for their lives.
And as for you...
Like I just said
One can only admire your commitment as a citizen.
But it was a tad egotistical too.
Be honest.
I mean, just imagine. They might've shot you.
A chain reaction.
You could have gone through lots of other transit points.
But NO.
YOU had to walk through the Brandenburg Gate.
You wanted to be famous for fifteen minutes, right?
And that's why you applied here to US.
Otherwise you wouldn't have applied to US at all.

Your egotism seriously jeopardised the glory of November
ninth, Peterchen.
(*Rounding things off.*) The policeman says sorry for being such
a coward.
You say sorry for being so stroppy.
Overtly political.
Spunky.

Pause.

Peterchen *suddenly starts to shriek repeatedly in short bursts like a
wounded animal.*
Viola *holds her tight.*

Viola (*in baby-talk*)   Oh poor you, you poor poor thing.
At long last you're getting rid of all the gunge. All that
grunged-down gunge. Yes, that's right, cry away. Just you
have a good cry. Nobody need be ashamed of tears,
Peterchen. Nobody on earth.
(*To herself.*) Your story's going to make you seriously rich.
You and the reconciled policeman. Splashed all over posters
up and down the country. There'll be millions in it.
(*Asking a question.*) A cognac?
First thing I'm going to do is make us both a colossal cognac.
How's that?

The lights in the room go down. Only the **Parrot***'s cage is still lit.*

The **Parrot** *makes sucking noises.*

Parrot (*asking a question*)   Hiya. Hiya. Don't I get a kiss
then?

It makes more sucking noises.

Blackout.

Round Two

Prologue without a theatre

In front of the curtain sits **Rosy**. *This time she is reading a tabloid newspaper. The props case is beside her. She is so immersed in her reading that she does not notice the audience taking their seats.*

The lights go down.

A spot on **Rosy**.

Rosy (*stands up*) Ah

She clears her throat and moves herself and her chair nearer the front edge of the stage.

Have you ever really thought about it? In the final analysis? (*Perplexed.*) In the final analysis you don't pay admission to a zoo for the ANIMALS but for the CAGE bars.

A long pause.

Nobody would dream of going to a zoo WITHOUT CAGE bars.

She shuffles even further upstage.

Only suicides.

A long pause.

She shuffles right to very front edge of the stage.

Pause.

(*Thinking hard.*) In the final analysis.
In the final analysis I think all punters have one thing in common.
(*Thinking hard.*) And that is –

Pause.

(*Thinking aloud.*) Yes, that's what it is. A longing, a deep longing to live WITH the wild animals

PEACEFULLY in the zoo
And WITHOUT any cages.

The curtain parts behind her.

*She is about to go back to her usual place but instead walks to the front
edge of the stage and stares at the audience.*

(*Sceptically.*) Outside the perimeter fence funnily enough
The punters are usually very proud of their cage bars.
They feel so guilty about the tiger

Pause.

(*Casually.*) That they overlook the whole zoo.

She runs to her place.

Scene Three

The dilapidated function room in the same hotel.
It is in the process of being renovated.
Upstage right a table on which are some non-alcoholic refreshments.
Tea and coffee.
To the left of this table the door to **Viola**'s *room.*
*In the back wall three windows. All three have been sealed with plans
for reconstruction.*
Upstage a leather sofa.
*Behind the sofa, hanging from the ceiling a large black and white photo
of Kalina de Sampinka in a bridal gown and Wim de Cuyp in a dinner-
suit. They are both standing in an Uncle Sam pose pointing at the
audience. The banner above them reads WE WANT YOU THE
SUGAR DOLLIES.*
Kalina is a young woman. Wim a drink-sodden fifty year-old.
A leather armchair.
Upholstered wooden chairs are scattered about the room.
Half-empty bottles and glasses litter the floor and the chairs.
In the left-hand wall – two plywood doors.
One has 00 on a sign above it.
The other says EXIT.
A fan on the ceiling.

On the sofa right **Peterchen** *sits smoking a cigarette.*

On her left sits **Babette** *in her Sunday best. Naturally she is just as fat as in Scene One. She is wearing an ocelot hat. On her lap there is a grey handbag. Near her, a check-pattern holdall. Around one hand is a white bandage. Hanging around her neck is a Lebkuchen heart on which SWEETHEART is written in icing sugar.*

To her left sits **Tabea**. *She has a bow in her hair and she is wearing a Dirndl skirt and brightly-coloured cheap glasses. She is still plump but noticeably slimmer than at the outset. A thread attached to her wrist holds a balloon.*

The festive clothes all four are wearing contrast with the building-site ambience of the room itself.

Rosy *sits down on the leather armchair and once again hides her face behind her tabloid newspaper.*

Viola *stands in the doorway.*

Peterchen, **Babette** *and* **Viola** *stare rigidly at the broken-down ceiling-fan.*

Tabea *gawps at the audience blankly and without expression.*

Peterchen   Funny that.
It was working just now.

Pause.

Babette   Dead right.

Viola (*impatiently*)   I mean, honestly.
(*To* **Peterchen**.) Get in.

Peterchen *gets up and nervously adjusts her clothing.*
Babette *nods at* **Peterchen** *and crosses the fingers of both hands in an over-friendly way.*
Peterchen *goes out into* **Viola**'s *room.*
Viola *stares at the others, shaking her head, and groans.*

The telephone tweets.

Viola   About bloody time, darling.

She closes the door behind her.

The instant the door shuts the fan creaks into motion once more.

Babette (*calling out*)   Oh, hello.
Are you there?
Hello, it's going again.
Bleeding fan.

Pause.

Got a mind of its own.
(*To* **Tabea**.) Don't you worry, angel. She'll be out of here
faster than YOU can count to five.

She sniffs the empty seat near her, then looks up again.

(*With an expression of disgust.*) EAST Berlin REALLY is a bit
different, eh.
Remember how Mum used to do charity work for nothing in
that reception centre camp.
(*Proudly.*) With her eyes closed our Babette could tell fifty
Easties APART by their smell alone.
Fifty of the buggers.

She has a sniff then looks up again.

EAST Berlin.

Rosy *briefly looks up over the top of her newspaper*.

Babette (*casually on the defensive*)   Yesterday, course, we had
this really incredible city tour, right.
(*Signalling dismissively.*) Seen a load of interesting
CORNERS.
Sort of stuff you don't never normally come ACROSS.
(*To* **Rosy** *in some surprise.*) In area, course, Dortmund's
bigger than Berlin.
(*Talking posh.*) Mainly of course as a result of the territorial
reforms.
There are some things here you just wouldn't think existed.
Hello there
Young woman
There YOU are.

Rosy (*curtly*)   I think so, yes.

Babette (*talking posh*)   It can only be a matter of moments now.

Pause.

(*To herself.*) Christ, I'm shit-scared.

She breathes deeply and thinks hard.

When you want to sing a folksong none come into your head.

Rosy *again peers over the top of her newspaper.*

Babette   A nice cool Babycham.
That's what I could do with right now.
How about YOU, Tabea?
Babycham for you, eh?
All the drinks on the table have gone.
Hmmm.

She picks up her bag.

But we're in luck, us two.

From her bag she takes out four different coloured Thermos flasks and puts them down in front of her.

Coffee. Milk. Knackwurst sausage. Colgate.
Yeaahh, your mum don't forget nothing.

Rosy *gets up and disappears in the ladies'.*
Babette *opens the lids of the first two flasks.*

Babette (*subdued*)   Has she made you LOSE your tongue, my treasure? You're not going all wimpish on me on the last leg, are you?
Come on, open your little beak, then.

Pause.

(*Asking a question.*) Just one little sip of Mummy's coffee.
THIS'LL make you feel bright-eyed and bushy-tailed.
Come on then, there's a good girl, Tabea, come on, come on.

As soon as **Babette** *puts the cup to* **Tabea**'s *lips she starts to retch silently as if about to choke to death any minute.*

(*Talking posh.*) Don't you worry yourself, treasure.

She opens the third flask.

(*Happily*.) This is the big one, so stand back.

In the flask is a bundle of sausages standing upright.

She eats a sausage.

NOTHING to touch these.
(*Menacingly*.) Tabea.
I'm telling you for your own good.
Open that gob of yours and say something.
Otherwise you'll get a back-hander in the face the LIKES
OF which YOU've never had from your mum before.
I swear THAT on my mother's grave.
If I have to bully you to be happy then bully you to be happy
I will.
And if you think any different YOU don't know me.

Rosy *comes out of the ladies' a little puzzled.*
Babette *takes* **Tabea**'s *hand, strokes it and nods to* **Rosy** *in a
mock-friendly way.*
Tabea *pulls her hand away.*

Rosy (*at the end of her tether*)   I've just dropped my last
hundred-mark note down the loo while I was peeing

She sits down.

I expect a rat will make itself a head-scarf out of it.

She goes on reading.

Babette   Four stones my daughter's lost for Wim de Cuyp.
(*Rapturously*.) Four stones.
Four stones, my daughter.

She turns back to **Tabea**.

Stopped at nothing, have you?
Stopped at nothing.
(*To* **Rosy**.) I wouldn't mind being one stone lighter neither.
You notice it when you climb stairs, you know.
(*Lying*.) But unfortunately
My doctor has STRICTLY forbidden me any diets on

health grounds.
(*Whinging.*) The trouble I have with my thyroids, my oh my.

Rosy *has not been listening.*

Rosy (*matter-of-fact*)   Does either of you ladies happen to be
a Scorpio?

Babette   Our Tabea was born on St Swithin's Day.

Rosy   NEVER sleep with a man if you don't know what his
mother looks like.

Pause.

Babette *gets up and gestures to* **Tabea** *that she should change places
with her. Then she takes toothpaste and a toothbrush out of her bag. She
opens the fourth Thermos from which steam rises. She then fills her
glass, brushes her teeth mechanically, gargles and spits the mouthwash
back. While doing this she keeps looking at* **Rosy** *in an irritated way.
Then* **Babette** *pours the other fluids back, switches all the lids around
and stows the Thermoses back in her bag.*

Babette (*during this procedure*)   YOU're loony, love. YOU
ought to go to Berlin. Where all the loonies are. That's where
you belong. (*She hums.*)

Rosy *folds her newspaper, sighs with relief, puts the paper back in her
props case, then looks into her pocket mirror.*

Rosy (*astonished*)   Wow, that's ME in there, I can see along
with MYSELF I'm gobsmacked, I really am.

Silence.

Babette (*defensively*)   Did you apply in writing, young
woman?

Rosy (*puts on lipstick*)   No.
I was approached in a department store.

Babette (*reassured*)   Ah, so you help display things, do you?

Rosy   I'd put it this way.
On the contrary.
I help destroy things.

I snap the aerials off of model tanks in the Toy Department.
Krrk.

She takes some aerials and Mercedes badges out of her case.

Here you are, see for yourself.

Babette (*hums once again*)   YOU'RE LOONY, LOVE.
(*Shocked.*) Just for fun, can I ask you what your DAY job is?

Rosy   I'm a cultural terroress.
I'm an actor.
To be honest, I'm an out-of-work actor.
I have a problem with the Fourth Wall.

She glances quickly at the audience.

Babette   With the what?

Rosy (*emphatically*)   WITH the Fourth Wall.
With the illusory bricks and mortar bit.

*She gets up and is about to go to the Fourth Wall but then decides
against her impulse and with a heavy heart she goes back to the window
wall.*

Imagine just for a moment
There are no windows here but only the auditorium
And WE're not on the seventh storey of a hotel but on the
stage.
(*Prattling.*) The aim common to all the people who
Might give me a part is that I should keep this Fourth Wall in
place
And my
Own personal aim is to

She takes up position.

Ensure that this Fourth Wall

She kicks in a window-pane.

IS shattered
Like that.

Babette *looks at the window-pane in dismay.*

Rosy   The people who
MIGHT
Give me work identify with the Fourth Wall.

Pause.

Bad luck for me.
Or bad luck for them.
Depending how you look at it.

She sits down again and goes on reading her book.

Pause.

Babette   And that's why you're out of work.

Rosy   DEAD right.
I'm allergic to Artistic Directors.
(*Irritated.*) Every male and female actor knows that fucking
the director means a guaranteed pension for every woman
actor over thirty-five.
Every male and every female actor knows that.
Why not just say it out loud then? WHY NOT?
In the past
Ogh
Way back in the early years of my unemployment I always
used to learn scripts by heart, closed my eyes and thought of
Brecht and Stanislavski.
TOTALLY BARMY.
Today I learn scripts by heart, close my eyes and think of my
clitoris.

Pause.

No director on earth can cope with a woman on stage not
thinking of Brecht and Stanislavski but worrying about her
orgasm instead.
No director on earth.
As I'm sure you kn –

She breaks off and looks quickly at **Babette**.

SENSING is BELIEVING. Every orgasm is a little dummy-
run for death.
(*Casually.*) As you can see I'm acting for dear life.

Oh yes, colleagues.
(*Pointing to* **Tabea** *and* **Babette**.) Acting for their pension.
Just guess, will you, who's causing most trouble in this
country?
(*Gently*.) But never mind.
(*She reassures herself with what she has just said*.) My two magic
words are DISTANCE and DISCIPLINE.
DISTANCE and DISCIPLINE are the OPEN SESAME to
a long-term contract.

She stands up.

I get up at crack of dawn with a High-ho, High-ho, It's off to
act we go.
I'm going to memorise Faust backwards BY denture-
therapy.
(*Clearly*.) I can sign-sing 'I Will Survive' and 'Silent Night'.
It underlines one's desire to communicate.

Goes across to **Tabea** *to express solidarity and gives her a
demonstration*.

(*Enthusiastically*.) AND all together now.

Tabea *does not react at all*.
Rosy *sits down again, deflated*.

Rosy   Maybe I should believe my analyst when she SAYS
my life is one long self-deception.

Pause.

I say the cinema in my head is more real than what my
analyst calls reality.

Pause.

(*Pointing to herself*.) Therapy-resistant.

A long pause.

(*Primly*.) I do hope that answers your question about my
DAY job to your entire satisfaction.
(*Groaning*.) Oghh, I've FINALLY got all that nervous
energy out of my system.

She starts reading her paperback again and hums brightly.

Pause.

Babette (*one syllable at a time*)   WHY are you here, please?

Rosy (*turned off*)   For the same reason I go to department stores.

Pause.

And anyway.

She takes a passport out of her jeans jacket.

My personal talent-passport expired this week.
Be my guest.
Once a year I VOLUNTEER to have my talent tested by the *PENTHESILEA* PERFORMANCE MOT UNIT.

She shows it to **Babette**.

Filled out and signed by Yours Truly.
I'm not mad.
I mean, my self-assessment might be well wide of the mark.
After all, my unemployment might be the result of a lack of talent.

She beats a drumroll on her props case.

(*Like a motto.*) But in next to no time the hurricane of hate which has been building up for millennia inside me will unleash itself on that Lower Bavarian Bimbo.
I shall
Shall suddenly and surprisingly break off in the midst of my most ferocious assault.

Breaks off her drumming and stares blankly ahead.

(*Concentrating.*) Break OFF.
Break off and get back in touch with my long lost innocence.

Pause.

Face to face with the tenderness of the tiger that bag of batter's ugly face will be reflected in MY pupils.
She will be reflected.

She drums.

Seen.

She drums.

Recognised.

She drums.

And then

She drums.

And then

She drums.

(*Casually.*) She'll be SICK.

Beats a final drumroll on the case.

(*Matter-of-fact.*) Let's shake on it. THE bet stands.

Takes out her sword and looks at it.

(*Sentimental and emotional.*) Today my long years of spear-carrying in the Amazon Army finally come to an end.
For the very last time I enlist in the battle for the Golden Straitjacket.
If I'm not absolutely mistaken, sweetheart, (*Looks at the Lebkuchen heart.*) THAT is your daughter over there, right?

Babette (*nods*)   Our Tabea.

Rosy   Can she hear what we're saying or is she (*She makes a gesture in sign language.*)?

Babette   If I can be COMPLETELY honest.

Rosy   For God's sake.

Babette (*falsely posh*)   Something ABSOLUTELY dreadful happened.

She pulls her away from **Tabea** *upstage.*

Last night after the city tour we came back to the hotel.
And out the window our Tabea saw the funfair with its Ferris wheel.
And the child got so one-track obsessed ABOUT the funfair

We went to see the floor show of the illusions.
Our Tabea was open-mouthed the WHOLE time.
Then she wanted to go to the rifle-range and win some fancy
feathers and a fox-tail to stick on her bike.
(*Astonished.*) Every shot a bull's eye.
So I say: What's this then, love, been having target practice
on the quiet?
No, she says, our Tabea is another William Tell.
And

She starts to cry.

Oh God, if only I'd known.
That big berk in the booth what had to reload the rifle
He gave the child such a funny sideways look and winked at
her
And our Tabea she
Winked her little eye back at him.
(*Enviously.*) I did think to myself: Something's wrong here.
Him with all them tattoos all up his arm
And me I'm wanting my bed
(*Categorically.*) NO, says MUMMY, no.
Just time for a quick look in the hall of mirrors THEN off to
beddy-byes.
If only I hadn't given in.

Pause.

And I notice soon as we go into the place THERE'S
something or someone there.
There's someone behind you, Babette.
So I turn round.

Pause.

(*Startled.*) There he is, the big berk with his tattoos
And just in front of me our Tabea.
Laughing and laughing fit to burst.
Getting thicker thinner thinner thicker smaller bigger bigger
smaller in the mirrors.
Then quick as a flash he grabbed the girl from behind and
dragged her down on the floor.

And I
I try to grab the balloon see
And rush
Headfirst with full force into the mirror.

She shows **Rosy** *her bandaged hand.*

Then all at once
(*In a panic.*) I see all the tattoos all up his arm.
The roses and the death's heads and the hearts.
Fatter thinner thinner thicker smaller bigger bigger smaller.
And I try to get him.
But all the time I'm getting deeper and deeper into my maze
of mirrors.
All I can see is MYSELF, just ME standing there.

Pause.

I must've been looking half an hour before I found the exit.
I go up to the caravan and knock.
And they rang the police right off.
A whole squad-carful piled IN to the maze of mirrors.
But our Tabea
She has vanished as if swallowed up by an earthquake.
The balloon just hangs there up against the ceiling.
And then at three that morning
We scoured the whole place.
The owner of the kiddies' carousel
Is just pulling the awning out over the carousel
And there the pair
Of them are sitting cool as cucumbers.
She's in her helicopter
And next to her in the fire-engine the big berk.
And the two of them calm-as-you-please smoking Peter
Stuyvesant.
And
And when her mum sees our Tabea with the BLEEDING
police out in force behind her
She rushes at me like a crazy and rips the balloon out my
hand and tries to smash her mum to a pulp.
But my friend and helper the Berlin bobby jumps in between

us and puts a headlock on her, the stupid sod.
Us two trot off down the station.
But from her
From that moment on
There's not another peep and she sort of squints at me
sideways.
And as for the big berk
They let the big berk go and nearly bring a charge against
me.

Pause.

At eight sharp I shot straight back to the hotel, had a shower
and packed my bags.
(*Lying.*) I say to her, Tabea, you don't have to say nothing
but if you still want to see Wim de Cuyp just slip on your
Dirndl, then your mum'll know.
(*Kitschily.*) And my daughter did slip on her Dirndl.
So then I knew.
Out the hotel by ten sharp.
Or we'd've had to pay an extra day.
And since eleven we've been sitting here, seven bleeding
hours more or less, waiting for our appointment at six.
But as for her
The girl hasn't said a word to her mum
TILL now
Not a sodding syllable.

She sits down beside **Tabea**.

(*Nods to* **Rosy**.) YOU hurry up mind, young woman.
We've got a night-train to catch.

Silence.

Rosy *looks at* **Tabea** *with horrified concern, is about to go over to her,
but then instead paces up and down the room and for a while doesn't
know what to do.*

Rosy (*shattered*)   That's
I mean that really is
(*Reproachfully.*) How COULD you at a time like this
Just before I'm due to go on

I MEAN REALLY YOU'VE GOT SUCH A FUCKING
nerve
A FUCKING nerve.

Pause.

Would you mind explaining to me how I'm going to go in
there and do *Penthesilea* in this state?
WOULD YOU MIND EXPLAINING THAT TO ME
PLEASE?

Pause.

But
(*Dismissively.*) Oh, what the fuck.
It's all my own fault.
ROSY, it's all your fault.
(*Reminding herself.*) DISTANCE and DISCIPLINE.
(*To* **Babette**.) DISTANCE and DISCIPLINE.
I should have known.
Fucking shit, how on earth am I going to get my
concentration back?
Fucking shit.

She sits down and has a very serious think.

Pause.

(*Distinctly.*) Cut.
That's it, cut something.
We'll just do a bit of a jump cut here.
Yeah, THAT's it.
(*To* **Babette**.) Listen to me.
I'm going to make you a one-off offer.
For you right now.
As a kind of public dress rehearsal if you like.
I'm going to do my *Penthesilea* just for you.

Pause.

What do you say?
Well, what do you say?
It'll help ME get my concentration back, it'll take your mind

off things and maybe your daughter's too.
Who knows?

*She takes sword and helmet out of her props case.
She brings out the pitbull terrier mask.*

(*Casually*.) Look, tell you what.
Why don't you
Why don't YOU join in?
You you can be the pitbull terrier.
Since the accident with my partner I do NOT on principle
work with amateurs any more but any port in a storm.

Pause.

Go on, go ahead.
Come on, come right over.
Come on.
There's no time to lose.
Go on then, go ahead.

Babette *gets to her feet, picks up the mask, notices something in the
case and bends down.*

Babette   What's this, then?

Rosy   That.
Oh, that.
That's something from a Job Creation Scheme.
That's a Hitler moustache.

Babette's *eyes light up.*

Rosy (*bored*)   OK, I'm EASY.
Far as I'm concerned you can do Hitler, if you like, I'm not
bothered either way any more.
You sit down on your sofa back there and be Hitler.
Just be Hitler.
Do what you want I'm sure it'll be fine.

She breaks off.

Or maybe the pitbull terrier after all.
Hmm.
You choose.

Right then.
Hitler or the pitbull terrier..

Babette, *feeling flattered, thinks it over rocking her head back and forth.*

Tabea (*very definite from the back*)   I'll be Hitler.

Babette (*calming her down*)   Noowah, I'm doing Hitler.

Tabea (*brooking no argument*)   No, our Tabea is doing Hitler.

Babette (*calming her down*)   Noowah, your mum is doing Hitler.

Tabea   NO, our Tabea.

Babette *turns around.*

Babette (*resolutely*)   NO, your –
(*Suddenly threatening.*) Hang on a minute, did someone speak?
Our Tabea's done a Lazarus, has she?
More seen than heard for hours on end.
Then jabbering away nineteen to the dozen.

Tabea (*resolutely*)   I'm doing Hitler.

Babette (*goes over to her*)   Just you look here, my girl.
What about the damage your mum done herself in the maze
of mirrors over you?
Eh, YOU don't say nothing more about that, I notice.

Tabea   I'm doing Hitler.

Babette   I am.

Rosy (*loudly*)   That's enough, you two. Shut up.

Pause.

We can't go on LIKE THIS.
If we're going to work together I draw the line at anything
that remotely resembles personalism.
(*Authoritarian.*) IS that clear?

Babette
Tabea } Certainly is.

Rosy (*to herself*)   Funny that EVERYBODY always wants
to do Hitler.
Though in fact in this case Hitler's a much less rewarding
role because it's a non-speaking part.
(*By way of suggestion to them both.*) The pitbull terrier's got
lines.

Pause.

Babette   I'm doing the pitbull terrier.

Tabea   I'm doing the pitbull terrier.

Babette   No, love, Mum's doing the pitbull terrier.

Tabea *barks*.

Rosy   OK, that's enough.
Look, we're going to approach this as true professionals.
TRUE professionals, all right?

She looks around the room.

Assuming that of all the people present in this room I've got
the most professional clout I'll decide who's playing what.
IS that clear?
Good.
Right.
Now you just stand there side by side please.

Babette and **Tabea** *stand side by side.*

Rosy (*explains very precisely with appropriate gestures*)   When I
say GO
YOU hold
(*To* **Babette**.) The moustache to your upper lip.
And YOU
(*Pointing to* **Tabea**.) Bark.
When I say SWITCH you hand over the moustache
And when I say GO YOU stick the moustache under your
nose and YOU bark.
Have you both got that?

Babette } Yep.
Tabea

Rosy   Brilliant.
We'll get to the mask in due course.

Pause.

OK.

Pause.

Now concentrate.
Right, on your marks. Ready steady

Pause.

GO.

Tabea *barks.*
Babette *positions herself as if delivering a military report, with her arms folded behind her, and stares with bulging eyeballs into the audience.*

Rosy   Lovely.
Very nice.
SWITCH.
And concentrate.

Pause.

GO.

Tabea *looks across at her mother and tries to do the same as her.*
Babette *looks at* **Tabea** *and makes a tweeting sound.*

Pause.

Rosy (*thrown by this*)   What was that supposed to be?

Pause.

(*To* **Babette**.) What did I say?
I said BARK not TWEET.
IS that clear?

Babette   Certainly is.

Tabea *barks at a different pitch.*

Pause.

Rosy *thinks it all over.*
Tabea *barks again at yet another pitch, snarls, then barks ecstatically.*
Babette *grabs the moustache.*

Babette   That doesn't count.
The girl's a animal-keeper.
I'm NOT playing no more.

Rosy (*bellowing*)   Stop it.
Quiet.
Stop it.
This is not a madhouse.
GO.
ON the sofa please and quiet.

She finds a chair and sits down to brood upstage left.

Tabea *and* **Babette** *look at her in rapt expectation.*

Rosy (*gestures to* **Tabea** *to come over*)   You.
Come over here a moment, will you?

Tabea *gets up, sticks her tongue out at her mother and crosses to* **Rosy**.

Rosy (*takes her hand*)   Now, what's your name, little girl?

Tabea   I'm our Tabea.

Rosy   Oh yes.
Of course.

She gestures to her to come closer.

(*Softly.*) I'm dead sure you've got more to offer than your mother but I've decided to cast the role against type.
(*Explaining.*) Your mother IS Hitler.
If you follow my meaning.
That's why she can't act him.
I think Hitler would be a big challenge for you. Precisely because you couldn't do it lying down.
(*Offering her her hand.*) I don't have a crystal ball handy but I'm certain we're going to have a very exciting working relationship.

Tabea *sits down again.*

Tabea (*to* **Babette**)   Up yours.

Rosy (*gestures* **Babette** *over*)   And what's your name?

Babette (*worried*)   Babette Mrugalla.

Rosy   Babette, love.
You have a quality of innocent fragility in your voice.
Do hold on to that.
It's a gift you're born with. You either have it or you don't.
YOU do have this quality.
It's my belief that playing the pitbull terrier bitch could
potentially be the role of your career.
(*Offering her her hand.*) I don't have a crystal ball handy but
I'm certain we're going to have a very exciting working
relationship.

Babette *returns to the sofa feeling a million dollars.*

Babette (*to* **Tabea**)   Nergh nergh to you.

Tabea (*to* **Babette**)   Nergh nergh to you.

Babette   And up yours.

Rosy *comes across to them with sword and helmet.*

Rosy (*to* **Tabea**)   You sit on the sofa under the wedding
photograph.
(*In passing.*) The toy balloon's got to go.

Tabea *ties the balloon to a chair-back.*
Rosy *ties the rope around* **Babette**'s *neck.*

Rosy   You.
You tweet at all the places underlined here.
ON your knees.

Babette *picks up the paperback and reads it.*
Rosy *opens her pocket-mirror and checks up on them both behind her by
looking in the mirror.*

Rosy   OK fine.
Tabea, a tad further left, please.
Lovely.

No no, hang on.
You've just stepped out of frame.
OK fine, love, stop.
Super.
OK fine.
Are we ready, loves?

Pause.

I can't hear anything.
ARE we ready?

Babette ⎱
Tabea ⎰ Ready.

Rosy (*to herself*)   Directing isn't the pushover I always
thought it was.
OK, now concentrate.

Pause.

(*Very concentrated and calm.*) HERE, Tigris, come to me, I need
you now. HERE, Leäne.

Suddenly very aggressive.

(*Violently.*) HERE, MELAMPUS, WITH YOUR LONG
AND MATTED HAIR.

Rosy *is performing very convincingly. Not badly.*
Babette *barks.*
Tabea *gives the Sieg Heil salute.*
Rosy *lowers the pocket-mirror and furiously yanks the leash so hard
that* **Babette** *falls flat on her face.*

Rosy   For Christ's sake, are you trying to make a complete
fool of me?

Babette (*hysterical*)   Look, come on, I only did what you
said I should do.

Rosy *furiously unbuckles the belt, hurls the helmet on to the floor and
sits back down on her chair.*
Babette *is about to sit down on the couch next to* **Tabea**.
Tabea *moves away from her and, still shaking her head, looks at her.*

Rosy (*turns back again to face them*)   WHAT did I say?

Pause.

WHAT did I say, Babette?

Babette (*emphatically*)   BARK.

Rosy (*blowing her top, she bears down on her*)   At the audition
you tweeted.
And that's why you got the part.
(*Dumbfounded.*) And now, now at the dress rehearsal you start
barking.

Pause.

(*Sitting down once more.*) Do you understand the difference
between TWEETING and BARKING?

Babette   Course.

Rosy   Evidently not.
Tabea, love, would YOU be an absolute angel and give your
colleague a demonstration of how to tweet?

Tabea *tweets*.

Babette (*bursts into tears*)   Doesn't count.
The girl's a animal-keeper.

Rosy *looks at her full of reproach*.
Babette *tweets very tentatively*.

Silence.

Rosy *stands up*.

Rosy (*very clearly*)   I SIMPLY DON'T BELIEVE THIS.
What the hell was THAT supposed to be?
I'm not interested in the fact that you can tweet.
I mean, I could easily cast a bird in your role.

Pause.

My God, do we have to start right from scratch?
THE BASIC SITUATION.
(*Prattling on.*) Penthesilea wants to let her dogs loose on the
person she loves because she thinks he has betrayed her.

You, the pitbull terrier bitch, feel in a purely intuitive way that Penthesilea is doing the wrong thing.
So, Babette, how do you react as the pitbull terrier bitch?

Pause.

Babette, love, are you listening?

Babette   Course.

Rosy   How do you as the pitbull terrier bitch react?

Babette *shrugs her shoulders.*

Rosy (*insistently*)   In order to survive you do the most natural thing in the world.

Pause.

You play-act.

Pause.

I mean, you're a woman after all.

Pause.

OK then.
(*Insistently.*) Your personality is split.
Is that too much to ask?

Pause.

(*She tries again.*) You think you're a bird.
A bird can't tear a person limb from limb, OK?
So you modify your conception of yourself.
You TWEET.
You TWEET.
And you rip Achilles apart as a bird.
THE person whom your mistress, namely YOU, are in love with.

Pause.

BUT afterwards you won't believe you've torn Achilles limb from limb.
Because as a bird you CANNOT tear a person limb from limb.
IS that clear?

Pause.

(*Reading her expression.*) No.

Pause.

(*She tries again insistently.*) What interests me is the split in you, OK.
The moment when this personality shift occurs, that's what you've got to show me.
I want to see the struggle.
The struggle.
Not the outcome.
Are you with me?
The struggle's what moves me.
The moment when everything's still open.
The moment when there's no going BACK.
That's what interests me.
Not the reality of whether you bark or tweet.
(*She groans.*) Right, OK.
We'll break off there.
Five minutes for coffee, loves, then we'll take it again from the top.

She gets up, looks for some coffee, but can't find any.

Fuck.

Quietly barking and tweeting in the background, **Tabea** *explains to* **Babette** *what* **Rosy** *means.*
Rosy *sits back down on her chair.*
Babette *notices that* **Rosy** *hasn't found any coffee and so generously crosses upstage holding her bag.*

Rosy (*rudely*)   Now what do YOU want? Oh really, do concentrate.

Babette *shows her the flasks in her bag.*

Rosy (*in passing*)   Keep that grey udder thing well away from me.
You might be able to lead your daughter up the garden path that way but NOT me.

She takes the flasks with their false lids out of the bag.

Here you are.
(*Matter-of-fact.*) You've switched all the liquids round.
Sausage, juice and coffee-grounds.
Mother's milk and toothpaste.
(*Distinctly.*) They're all as dry as the Gobi desert.
(*Caustically.*) NEVER but NEVER EVER try that on me
again, OK?
IS that clear?

Pause.

NEVER ever.

Pause.

Right, let's GO for it.
TO your position and wait till you're called.

Babette *draws back bent double.*

Rosy (*drawling*)   Tabea, come over here a minute, will you?

Tabea *gets up nervously and takes up position beside her.*

Rosy (*puts her arm around her shoulders and nods to her*)   Not
bad.
Not bad.
(*With real concern.*) But what you're doing is still just a touch
transparent, know what I mean?
In THIS context what really interests me is not Hitler the
historical personage, OK?

Tabea *gives her a blank look.*

Rosy (*reading her expression*)   How can I best explain it to
you?

Pause.

Playing Hitler nowadays you need two aims at once: to be
omnipresent yet still invisible.

She looks straight at her.

HITLER realism if you like.
(*Reading **Tabea**'s expression.*) No, you don't follow me, do you?
Oh, fuckit fuckit, how can I explain it to you?

Pause.

(*Gives the Sieg Heil salute.*) All that stuff is just cliché history-book Hitlerism.

She removes her moustache.

And all that is pure fancy dress.
But I'm talking about the truth.

Looks her in the face.

No, you still don't see.
If you want to act Hitler on stage you mustn't make any distinction between GOOD and EVIL, between victims and (*Interrupts herself.*) I can see you don't see.

A long pause.

Tabea, listen to me.
I'm going to do something I've never done in my whole life.
I'm going to confide the deepest secret of the theatre to you.
That's what I'm going to do.
Don't ask me why.
But I believe, yes believe, YOU and YOU alone deserve to know the truth.

Pause.

(*Very gently.*) Do you want to hear it, Tabea?
Think about it.

Tabea (*breaking the mood, stupidly*)   Oh yeah, I WANT to hear THAT.

Rosy (*sits* **Tabea** *down on her lap*)   You're acting a part on stage.
The performance is over.
You hang your costume in your dressing-room.

Pause.

Is the part dead then?

Tabea   Nah.

Rosy   Are YOU dead?

Tabea   Nah.

Rosy   Would you be dead if you had NOT been playing the part?

Tabea   Nah.

Rosy   Would the part be dead if you'd NEVER played it?

Tabea   Nah.

Pause.

Rosy (*matter-of-fact*)   You're NEVER dead, do you see?
You're ALWAYS there.
No matter what part you're playing.
Even if you're not playing any part. Every story that has an ending is a lie.

Tabea *nods.*

Rosy   And now, Tabea.
Tell me WHAT the truth is.

Tabea (*taking off her glasses, very quietly*)   Love.

Rosy *kisses* **Tabea** *on the forehead.*

Rosy (*very matter-of-fact*)   And knowing all this I want YOU and YOU alone to PLAY Hitler.

Lets her go and gets up herself.

Tabea *follows her.*

Rosy *and* **Tabea** *are standing next to each other.* **Rosy** *is concentrating as if she wanted to send her own thoughts to* **Tabea**.
Rosy *holds out her plastic sword.*

Rosy (*to herself, thinking hard*)   We've got to chop the guilt up into bits.
As long as you go on believing in guilt you'll stay a puppet manipulated by Babette Mrugalla.
Until men learn to share their power, all of us, every single one of us, the whole world, will stay hostages of the enchanted queens.
(*Tries to understand herself while talking.*) As long as we don't

chop the guilt up into bits we'll never experience that. If the truth be told each one of us human beings is God.
(*Easy*.) God.
God who plays sweeper in his own final.
(*Smiles*.) And who's forgotten
After five minutes
That he is God
(*Shrugging her shoulders*.) Believing instead he's team sweeper.
Can you sense its presence here? (*Without touching* **Tabea**'s *forehead*.)
A sort of radiant blue ball
Full of light.
Our heritage is the mote in this ball but the truth is the ball.

Silence.

Tabea *starts singing* '*My Way*' *in fantasy Russian.*

Rosy *puts down her sword and goes back to the chair without watching* **Tabea**. **Rosy** *is exhausted and wipes sweat off her forehead. During all this she casually but without interruption sings* '*I Will Survive*' *in sign language.*

Babette *watches* **Tabea** *and* **Rosy**. *She looks very insecure. Finally she gets up. She expects a directing note from* **Rosy**. *As* **Rosy** *is not giving her any attention she decides to do something on her own. She puts the pitbull terrier mask on and, shrugging her shoulders, gives the Sieg Heil salute.*

The door opens.

In the doorway **Viola** *stands, holding a brandy glass, with her other arm draped around* **Peterchen**'s *shoulder.*

Babette *runs to the hole in the window-pane.*

Tabea *is quiet again.*

Rosy *looks in the direction of the door.*

Peterchen *has calmed down but still seems exhausted and mechanical.*

The ceiling-fan stops.

Viola We've obviously been having a lovely time.

Rosy   How come LOVELY?
(*Looking at* **Viola**.) And how come WE?

Viola (*asking a question*)   Are you next?

Rosy (*detaching herself from* **Tabea**)   Certainly am.

Viola   Well, do get going.
I'm way behind schedule.

Rosy   You can say THAT again. (*Winking at* **Tabea**.)
(*Looks at* **Viola** *and sizes her up*.) I need a minute at most.
(*Picking up helmet and sword*.)

Viola (*to* **Peterchen**)   Now you just think it over, will you?
I'd really go for it in a big way.

Peterchen *does not respond.*

Viola   I've got your phone number.
I'll give you a bell early next week, then.
(*Holding out her hand*.) And lots of love to your kiddies.

She looks doubtfully at **Rosy** *who is standing ready and then
disappears into her room.*
Rosy, *standing in the doorway, turns around once more.*

Let's shake on it. THE bet stands.

Viola*'s door shuts.*
Babette, *with her mask on her head, rushes to the keyhole and peers in.*
Peterchen *stays standing in the room, indecisively staring at the
exit, and is about to light a cigarette. The packet is empty. She sits down
in* **Rosy***'s place and watches what is going on in the room.*

Babette   Oh my God.

Retches.

Oh my God.
You just can't look. People CANNOT do that.

Retches.

Oh my God.

She moves quickly away from the keyhole, pulls off the mask and sits down on the couch with her face averted from the door.
Tabea *walks calmly up to the door.*

Tabea   You can't afford to be too soft, Mum.

She kneels down peering and gulping.

The door flies open. **Tabea** *is thrown against the wall. With her hand over her mouth,* **Viola** *runs to the ladies' vomiting.*

Silence.

Tabea *creeps out from behind the door, stands up straight and positions herself in line with the door.*
Rosy *strides calmly out through the door, slowly removes her helmet, unbuckles her belt and takes her talent passport and a pencil from her jeans jacket.*

Rosy   Right.
(*Signing her card.*) Extended for another year
If I've judged the lady aright she'll be available again in about five minutes.
(*To* **Babette**.) You can keep the mask by the way.
I've got all the hate out of my system now.

She starts to pack her things back into her case.

A peculiar sort of tension develops between **Rosy** *and* **Peterchen**.
Rosy *looks up carefully.*

Tell me something.
Haven't we met somewhere before?

Peterchen *carefully gets up from her chair and then makes the victory sign.*
Rosy *carefully gets up and does the same.*
Rosy *and* **Peterchen** *feel like hugging each other. But somehow can't.*

Rosy   How have you been all this time?

Peterchen   I think I can best sum it up by saying
Gulp Gasp.

Rosy   And your boyfriend.
How's he?

Peterchen   Reading porno mags and eating fruit from the
South.
But we've split up now.

Pause.

And what about your boyfriend, has he still got green hair?

Rosy *laughs.*

Rosy   No, right now I don't think he's got any.

Silence.

And how's your son?
(*Asking a question.*) Rico?

Peterchen   Ricardo.
Ricardo is learning to drum.

Silence.

Rosy   Right.
(*Non-committally.*) I must be on my way. Got another date
with myself in quarter of an hour.

She is about to go.

Viola *comes out of the ladies' bent double with a handkerchief over her
mouth. The ceiling-fan stops.*

Viola (*clears her throat, applies lipstick to her mouth, then looks
daggers at* **Rosy**)   I never want to see you again in my life.

Rosy *snaps her fingers casually and without letting herself be
distracted in the direction of the ceiling-fan which immediately starts
whirring again.*

Rosy   I seem to have heard that somewhere before.

*She stands in the exit door a few moments and turns around again
briefly.*

Your entrance, Tabea.

Blackout.

Variant or

Epilogue in the theatre

A glowing red sunset.
The conference room.
The window with its plastic blinds rolled up.
In the background the lit-up Reichstag.
On the writing-desk the colour television set showing a close-up of **Rosy**'*s hate-contorted face.*

Tabea *is kneeling on the desk.*

Viola *is glued to her desk chair in dismay.*

Babette *is sitting to the right of the* **Parrot**'*s cage. She is enthusiastically playing the mouth-organ. The violet balloon is attached to the chair backrest.*

The **Parrot** *is rocking back and forth in its cage.*

Tabea (*sings rapturously*)   The Mrugallas are as lucky as hell.
So far everything has turned out well.
And they belong together.

She discovers the hand-fan and fans air into **Viola**'*s face.* **Viola** *cringes.*

Babette ⎫
Tabea ⎭ Like the wind and the sea.

Viola *picks up the hand-fan, examines it, tries to switch it on again but it doesn't work.*

Tabea   Tabea loves Michael.

Babette   And Tabea loves me.

Tabea *breaks off, turns the swivel-chair round the wrong way to face* **Viola** *frontally and gives her a challenging look.*

Babette *finishes her mouth-organ playing on a high note waiting for a round of applause.*

A short silence.
The **Parrot** *sways again, then jabbers.*
Viola *turns on the* **Parrot** *reproachfully.*
The **Parrot** *croaks furiously, then goes quiet.*

Tabea   Personally I do NOT have any HANG-UPS.

Babette *gives* **Viola** *an expectant look.*

Viola (*bangs her file shut*)   Don't call us.
Thank you for your time.
Now all you have to do is sign here and that's that for the
moment.

Pause.

Babette   WHAT?
What?
That went fast all of a sudden.

Viola (*clearing her desk, curtly*)   Right.
SO fast all of a sudden.

Pause.

You see that door over there. That's the Exit.

Babette *gets up and stands there in the room, helpless.*

Viola   And please
Before you go into the lounge
Do yourselves and me a major major favour and release your
(*Pointing with disgust at* **Tabea**.) ravaged daughter from that
moustache.

Silence.

Tabea   This isn't going to work, Mum.
I vote we clear off out of here fast.

Starts to get up.

Babette *pushes her back into the armchair.*

Babette (*perplexed*)   What has she done wrong?
She hasn't done nothing wrong, has she?
Tabea, have you done something wrong?

Tabea   I'm the girl with no name. I know nothing.

Viola (*with conviction*)   Closing credits.
It's time for the closing credits.
Over finished period stop end of transmission closing credits.
And now out of here fast out out out.

Babette (*disoriented*)   What what tone of voice is she
suddenly talking to me in?

Viola *goes to the door and opens it.*

Viola   We'll write to you with our decision.

Silence.

Babette   Miss, please. Miss, please.
Five

Crosses to **Viola** *and kisses her hand.*

Five five five minutes please.

Viola (*pulls her hand away*)   Stop this nonsense at once.

Babette   FOUR
FOUR
Four minutes.

Viola   Stop this at once.

Babette   Please.

Pause.

Please.

Pause.

Please.

Viola *takes a deep breath, then retreats to her desk chair.*

Babette   Come on now, Tabea, let your mum sit down
here a minute. Come on now come on come on.

Tabea (*stubbornly*)   I want to be out of here like double
quick, OK.

Babette   In a mo, my angel, in a mo.
You sit down here a minute next to Mum.

Come on now.
Come on.

Tabea *wants to sit in* **Babette**'s *place.*

Babette (*looking at* **Viola**)   And
That moustache.
Take that idiot moustache off, girl.

Tabea   Nah, not going to, so there.

Babette   THEY MUST'VE SHAT IN YOUR BRAIN
OR SOMETHING.

Viola (*calmly*)   THREE minutes.

Babette   Let US be off home then.

Sits down opposite **Viola**.

Tabea *sits down on* **Babette**'s *chair and follows what happens with
rapt concentration.*

Babette (*in a businesslike manner*)   There's just one teeny
weeny problem here.

She shuffles closer and whispers behind her outstretched hand.

The neighbours.

Viola *doesn't respond.*

Babette (*goes on whispering*)   I've already let all the
neighbours know.
Let them know that our Tabea's appearing on the Wim de
Cuyp show.
And now she's not.

Pause.

So what we going to do about it, Miss?
They'll laugh like bloody drains.

Viola   Two.

Babette   Sorry.

Viola *leans back.*

Viola   In your opinion, WHAT should I accept your daughter as in this blind date show?

Babette (*thinking hard*)   How about a senior citizens angle?

Viola   How about a Handicapped Half Hour?

Pause.

Tabea (*thinks hard for a moment, then very quietly*)   I'm going to smash YOU one right in the gob, you stupid bitch.

Babette (*whispering*)   SHUT your mouth, you.

Viola (*pulls herself together*)   My dear Frau Mrugalla, let's bring this discussion to a dignified conclusion, shall we?

Pause.

You're wasting your time.
Your daughter will not appear on *Sugar Dollies*.
Never.
Ever.
Never.
Do you catch my drift?
Ever.

Babette *gets up without saying a word, goes across to her shopping-basket, takes out a preserving-jar and puts it down on* **Viola**'s *desk.*

Babette   And what about this?

Viola   What about what?

Babette   Four stones.

Tabea *screws up her face in disgust.*

Babette   Four stones for the Wim de Cuyp show.
Have I saved all this just to chuck it away?

Viola   I'm sorry, I don't follow.

Babette   She's got a hundred jars of puke in her room.
ONE next to the other.
I mean she's got jars for Wim de Cuyp and Kalina de Sampinka up to the ceiling.

Up to the ceiling, she has.
The first fifty jars have got a bit mouldy by now.

Viola   Take it off my desk at once.

Babette   Temper justice with mercy.

Pause.

Go on.

Pause.

Please.

Viola (*gets to her feet and picks up the telephone*)   Unless you leave this room at once I'm calling security.

Babette (*takes a chequebook out of her pocket, picks up* **Viola***'s passport and reads from it*)   What will make you sit up and take notice, girl?
(*Reading aloud.*) Fiola.
(*Writing.*) Three thousand.
Is three thousand enough?

Viola (*quietly*)   Out.

Babette   OK fine.
People who do a lot can offer a lot.
(*Writing.*) Promise to bear the payer
Five thousand.
My pleasure.

She gives her the cheque and then picks up a form.

Right and now we make a little cross here.
SIGNED Tabea Mrugalla.

She opens her bag.

Swap the photo of Lydia for the one of our Tabea
And Bob's your uncle.

Viola (*dialling a number*)   Hello, security please.

Babette (*unimpressed*)   Give me that phone a minute, will you?

Viola *refuses to do so.*

Babette   Give me that phone.
This has gone beyond a joke, girl.
The phone.

Viola   I'm warning you.

Babette   And quick about it.

Parrot   Hiya.

Viola   And YOU're straight down the garbage disposal,
you fucking bitch.

Tabea (*automatically*)   Well, you can't afford to be too soft,
Mum.

*She gets up, goes across to the desk, picks up the hand-fan, opens the
parrot cage and holds the fan inside.*
*The **Parrot** jabbers in panic.*
Viola *and* **Babette** *wrestle without noticing what* **Tabea** *is doing
with the telephone.*

Viola   Leave my Handyfone alone.

Tabea (*considerate*)   Oh, you speak French, do you, can I
drink sherry with you por favor.

Viola   Leave my Handyfone alone.

Babette   Ch-andy Ch-andy Ch-andy I'll show you ch-ow
ch-andy it is.

*Holding it in her hand she discovers the window is open and is about to
pitch it out.*

Tabea (*in a monotone*)   Have sherry with you por favor.

Viola (*clutches **Babette**'s hand tight*)   I'll have you locked
up, you antisocial peasant.

Babette (*punching at her face like a boxer*)   You're going to see
a different side of me now.

Babette *punches her again. They wrestle and bump into the TV set.*
The picture goes on running.

Rosy   Trample underfoot the ranks of men.
Bring your bronze chariot down to me.
Let me set my foot upon his throat.

Babette (*punches*)   Think you're superior or something, do
you?

Rosy   Seize the wings and travel through the fields.

Babette (*punches*)   I didn't take to you from the start.

Rosy   And like a thunderbolt from stormy clouds.

Babette (*punches*)   From the very start.

Rosy   Fall upon this Grecian's skull.

On the screen we see **Viola** *running out with her hand held over her
face.* **Rosy** *shrugs her shoulders in astonishment. The video spools
back on fast rewind. We see* **Peterchen** *flickering on the screen.*

Viola (*out of breath*)   Antisocial peasant.

Babette   Let the Ch-andy alone or I'll do for you.
I'll do for you.
I'll do for you.

The **Parrot** *goes on jabbering, undeterred.* **Tabea** *continues to hold
the hand-fan in its cage and looks at the other two.*

Tabea (*in a monotone*)   Ch-ave sherry with you por favor.

Babette   Or I'll do for you.

All of a sudden, **Babette** *grabs* **Viola** *by the legs.* **Viola** *half hangs
out of the window.*

Viola   No, don't.
Please don't. I have a family.

Babette   Love thy neighbour, that's where you're going
wrong.

Babette *lets* **Viola** *go.*

Viola *plunges down without a sound.* **Babette** *bends over to look and
watches her fall. Then without any qualms she shuts the window.*

The **Telephone** *tweets.*

Telephone   Security here.

Babette *switches it off, lifts the dish-cover, has a good sniff, puts her plate on the desk, fills a glass with champagne and starts to eat.*

Tabea *takes her hand out of the cage. The* **Parrot** *is dead. The hand-fan works again.*

Silence.

Tabea   If you're feeling bruised and bad

Babette (*chiming in*)   We'll make sure you don't stay sad.

She goes on eating.

Tabea *walks like an automaton to the window and peers down.*

Tabea   Blue ball here
Or blue ball there
Viola's flat out in the square.

She looks up to the ceiling.

The ceiling-fan starts turning again.

Babette   Come on, pile everything on your plate, Tabea.
Stuff your guts full.
For the next few years we'll only be getting tap water and dry bread.

Silence.

Tabea *is still peering down.*

Tabea (*paralysed*)   You'll be stuck in jail now, Mum.
You'll have to sew mailbags till your last hour strikes.

Babette   In on the crime – help do the time.

Tabea (*in a monotone*)   If YOU think I'm going to smuggle a file into your cell inside a raisin cake you must be right off your head.
You got yourself into THIS shit, so you can shovel yourself out again.

Babette (*undeterred, she goes on filling her face*)   I knew from the very start you was as evil as the day is long.

Tabea (*in a monotone*)   I'm off home on my own now. I'll pack up my bits and bobs, give my notice to my boss and to Chico at the rifle-range (*Talking posh.*) You won't see me for dust.

Babette   You'll fall under a bus, you silly cow.

Tabea   And I will change completely from top to bottom like that mad bitch said
(*Menacingly.*) I swear THAT on my MOTHER'S GRAVE.

Babette   Anyone what really wants to CHANGE, Tabea, CAN'T have been much cop to start with.

Tabea (*reaches out her hand, talking posh and very solemnly*)   Let us part in peace.

Babette *goes on filling her face and ignores her.*
Tabea *is about to leave, then comes back uncertainly, crosses to her chair and ties her balloon to her mother's chair-back.*

Tabea (*cautiously*)   Mum.

Pause.

(*Asking a question.*) Love?

Pause.

Love.

Babette (*bitterly*)   Yes, Tabea, I know.

Tabea *and* **Babette** *exchange looks.*

Babette   I know.

At that moment two **Policemen** *sidle through the door into the room. They both have a bandage around their hands and point their pistols at* **Tabea** *and* **Babette**.

Babette (*curtly*)   Oh no, THAT PAIR again.

A crisp blackout.

**The Gate Theatre presents
the British Premiere of**

After the Rain

by Sergi Belbel

**translated by Xavier Rodríguez Rosell,
David George and John London**

cast

Head of Administration	Nicholas Boulton
Blonde Secretary	Clare Cathcart
Red-Haired Secretary	Ester Coles
Local Messenger	Charlie Condou
Computer Programmer	Steven Elder
Managing Director	Ingrid Lacey
Brown-Haired Secretary	Bonnie Engstrom
Dark-Haired Secretary	Julie Markey
Director	Gaynor Macfarlane
Designer	Francis Gallop
Costumes	Johanna Coe
Production Manager	Vian Curtis
Production Assistant	Jane Wolfson
Stage Manager	David Warwick
Assistant Stage Manager	Chris Gill

for the Biennale

Artistic Director	David Farr
Producer	Rose Garnett
Project Co-ordinator	Clare Goddard
Manager	Karen Hopkins
Literary Supervisor	Joy Lo Dico
Production Co-ordinator	Melissa Naylor
Press Officer	Rachel Stafford

After the Rain is generously supported by the Spanish
Embassy.

Biographies

Sergi Belbel (Writer)
Although born in 1963 into a Spanish-speaking family, he has concentrated on Catalan to such an extent that the Catalan daily *Avui* said, 'Catalan Theatre is called Sergi Belbel.' In 1985 he won the Marqués de Bradomin Prize for **A.G/V.W. Calidoscopis i fars d'avui** (A.G./V.W. Kaleidoscopes and Lighthouses of Today). He has also translated and directed plays from English and French. His plays have included the monologue **La nit de cigne** (The Night of the Swan, 1986) and the two-hander **En companyia d'abisme** (Deep Down, 1988), both significant for their manipulation of language, fragmentation of narration and experimentation with form. He continues this exploration with **Dins la seva memòria** (Within His Memory, 1987), **Tálem** (The Marriage Bed, 1989), and **Caricies** (Caresses, 1991), which have all earned him the reputation of being at the forefront of Catalan and Spanish avant-garde drama.

Nicholas Boulton (Head of Administration)
Trained at Guildhall School of Music and Drama. Theatre includes **The New Menoza** (Gate Theatre), the lead in **Antonio's Revenge** (Chelsea Arts Centre), **Arcadia** (Michael Codron Ltd, Haymarket Theatre) and **An Ideal Husband** (Salisbury Playhouse). Television includes **Two Golden Balls** and **Under the Moon** (BBC).

Clare Cathcart (Blonde Secretary)
Theatre includes **The Party's Over** (Nottingham Playhouse), **Translations** (Donmar Warehouse), **Venetian Twins** and **Fooling About** (Oxford Stage Company), **Cloud Nine** and **The Duchess of Malfi** (Contact Theatre), **Same Old Moon** (Gielgud), **Crucible** (NT), **The Sash** (7:84) and **Joyriders** (Paines Plough). Television includes **Casualty**, **Over Here**, **Searching**, **Father Ted**, **Goodnight Sweetheart**, **Paris**, **The Bill**, **Rides**, **Lovejoy**, and **Lost Belongings**. Film includes **Big Pants**. She has also done extensive radio work including **Eamon**, **Older Brother of Jesus**.

Johanna Coe (Costumes)
Trained at Bradford University in Art, Fashion and Textiles. Theatre includes **Der Leser**, **Das Tier** and **Die Bucklige**. (Theater der Stadt, Heidelberg), **Wild Tales**, **The Tempest**, and **A Picture of Dorian Grey** (BAC), **A Show of Hands** (a deaf-

signing company), work with Theatre de Complicite includes **The Street of Crocodiles**, **Three Lives of Lucie Cabrol** (including world tours) and **Out of a House Walked a Man** (Lyttleton, RNT). Forthcoming work includes **Endgame** (Donmar Warehouse).

Esther Coles (Red-Haired Secretary)
Trained at RADA. Work at RADA includes **The Bacchae**, **A Family Album**, **Wild Honey**, **Kasimir and Karoline**, **Amongst Barbarians**, **A Midsummer Night's Dream** and **London Cuckolds**. Theatre includes **Can't Stand Up For Falling Down**, **Woyzeck** and **The Snow Queen** (Hull Truck Theatre Company) and **The Recruiting Officer** (Royal Exchange Theatre). Television includes **Bad Girl**, **Resnick**, **Coronation Street** and **Peak Practice**.

Charlie Condou (Local Messenger)
Films include **Judge Dredd** and **To Kill a Priest**. Television includes **Pie in the Sky**, David in **Martin Chuzzlewit**, **Frank Stubbs Promotes** and **Frank Stubbs 2**.

Vian Curtis (Production Manager)
Resident Production Manager at the Gate. Trained at RADA. Theatre includes **Bloodknot** and **Don Juan Comes Back From the War** (Gate), **Heart and Sole** (Gilded Balloon/Newcastle Comedy festival), **So You Think You're Funny?!** (Gilded Balloon), **The Lottery Ticket** (BAC and Pleasance), carpenter for Hilton Productions and **Miss Julie** (New End Theatre, Hampstead).

Steven Elder (Computer Programmer)
Trained at Webber Douglas. Theatre includes **Macbeth** (Lyric Hammersmith and tour), **Disappeared** (Leicester Haymarket and tour), **The Case of Rebellious Susan** (Orange Tree Theatre), **Comforting Myths** and **The Green Parakeet** for the Greenwich Studio Theatre; a national tour of **Measure for Measure**, **Macbeth** at the New End Theatre and a season with Southwold Repertory. Steven has also played the title role in **Hamlet** for Made-up Theatre Company and for Buttonhole Theatre Company. Screenwork includes **Suffer the Little Children** and **Resnick**.

Bonnie Engstrom (Brown-Haired Secretary)
Trained at the Guildhall School of Music and Drama. Theatre
includes Ariel in **The Tempest**, Young Woman in Edward Bond's
Bingo (RSC). Film includes Louise in **True Blue**.

Frances Gallop (Designer)
Recent work includes **Bretevski Street** (Birmingham Rep), **The
Gowk Storm** and **Oedipus Tyrannos** (Royal Lyceum,
Edinburgh), **The Albright Fellow** (Fifth Estate), **Just Whores**
and **Crashing** (Radge Theatre). A self-proclaimed 'Engineer of
the Fantastic', he has managed theatrical happenings with
Ridgeway Theatre, The Passion Plays, Welfare State
International, Lord Dynamite and is currently working on two
American tours for the Haworth Shakespeare Festival, New Jersey.

**David George, John London and Xavier Rodríguez Rosell
(Translators)**
David George and John London teach Spanish and Catalan at the
University of Wales, Swansea and have published **Contemporary
Catalan Theatre: An Introduction**. Xavier Rodríguez Rosell is
a graduate of the Faculty of Translation and Interpreting at the
Autonomous University of Barcelona and studied at the University
of Wales, Swansea from 1993 to 1994.

Ingrid Lacey (Managing Director)
She is best known for her role as Helen Cooper in **Drop the Dead
Donkey**. She has also appeared in **A Woman's Guide To
Adultery**, **The Chief**, **Master of the Moor**, **Inspector Morse**,
London's Burning, **Northanger Abbey**, **Never Come Back**,
The Bill, **Pie in the Sky**, **Strathblair** and **Saracen**. Theatre
includes Bristol Old Vic, Manchester Contact Theatre, Watermill,
Oldham Coliseum and Derby Playhouse.

Julie Markey (Dark-Haired Secretary)
Theatre includes Olivia in **Twelfth Night**, Tante Moirel in **Les
Grand Meauines**, **Newsrevue** (Canal Café Theatre) Ylena in
The Wood Drum.

David Warwick (Stage Manager)
During the six years he has worked in theatre his experience has
covered most aspects of theatre production, from lighting for
Macbeth and pantomimes, to making oversized props for
Godspell, then having to sit in the band pit and throw up props to
the actors on stage. Recently worked on productions of **Natural**

Causes and **Time and Time Again** at the Victor Graham
Comedy and Drama Season, in Ayr and toured as stage manager
with 2 TIE projects.

Jane Wolfson (Production Assistant)
Theatre includes Assistant Director on **The Land of the Living**
(Royal Court), **Playhouse Creatures** (Sphinx Theatre
Company), **The Cheating Hearts** (Gate) and **Pig Voice** (Pop-
up Theatre Company). Also worked as Assistant Manager of the
Gate for 18 months and currently Producer of Pop-up Theatre
Company.

After the Rain

Sergi Belbel

Translation by Xavier Rodríguez Rosell, David George
& John London

Characters

The employees of a finance company (one of the four or five which occupy the building):

Computer Programmer
Head of Administration
Blonde Secretary
Dark-Haired Secretary
Red-Haired Secretary
Brown-Haired Secretary
Local Messenger
Female Managing Director

Place: Roof of a forty-nine storey skyscraper, an intelligent office building of high standing. A leaden sky without the threat of rain.

Time: The present or the near future.

This text went to press before the opening night and may therefore differ from the version as performed.

Scene 1

The **Head of Administration** *and the* **Computer Programmer** *step out onto the roof discreetly.*

Head of Administration   Here.

Computer Programmer   It's too cold.

Head of Administration   As long as it's not windy . . .

Computer Programmer   Or rainy . . .

Head of Administration   What?

Computer Programmer   No, no, of course, that's impossible, it was . . . a joke.

Head of Administration   After all this time . . . Two years already, isn't it? Perhaps even more. That would be too much, don't you think? Two years without rain and today of all days, it would . . . No, no, don't worry. It would have appeared on the front page of every newspaper.

Computer Programmer   And they won't tell us anything, up here?

Head of Administration   No.

Computer Programmer   What if they see us? What if they . . . find us?

Head of Administration   Who?

Computer Programmer   Someone could come up.

Head of Administration   If anybody came, it would be to do the same thing we're doing.

Computer Programmer   Oh. Perhaps. I hadn't thought about it. But, perhaps not.

Head of Administration   It wouldn't be the first time.

Computer Programmer   Has it always been banned?

Head of Administration   Yes. From the day the Company started.

Computer Programmer   I mean, for the staff of the
Company. Before you were transferred here, for example.

Head of Administration   Before? No, it wasn't allowed
either. But there weren't any rigorous inspections. Not at the
entrance, or in the toilets or the cafeteria.

Computer Programmer   So you say you know
somebody who's come up here to . . .

Head of Administration   Yes. Well, I've never seen
them, but I've got a good idea who they are.

Computer Programmer   How do you know?

Head of Administration   I've got a good sense of smell.
For breath.

Computer Programmer   I see.

Head of Administration   By the way, I'd never have
imagined that you . . .

Computer Programmer   Well, I do. I'm a bit ashamed
to admit it, but I do.

Head of Administration   My sense of smell didn't work
with you. Ashamed, you said?

Computer Programmer   I've been hiding it well. I don't
know how I have been able to restrain myself so much.

Head of Administration   Is it your first time, today?

Computer Programmer   Yes. During working hours, it
is.

Head of Administration   Three months restraining
yourself for so many hours, that's quite a lot. I mean, you've
been here for three months, haven't you?

Computer Programmer   Yes. I've been controlling
myself. That's why I get so nervous sometimes. Especially
with these annoying men and women bothering me with
their questions all the time. I mean the secretaries. Especially
them.

Head of Administration   I see. Well, that's enough, come on, quick, before they realize we're missing.

The **Head of Administration** *takes out two cigarettes from a little silver case and a lighter. The* **Computer Programmer** *looks around nervously.*

Computer Programmer   I think it's too windy, we won't be able to light them, besides, you're right, it's horrible when it's windy, I mean, you don't feel like it at all, obviously I always feel like it, especially when it's forbidden, like here, like now, but maybe we should go down, you said so yourself, they'll realize we're missing and somebody'll be suspicious, if we're not in the cafeteria . . .

Head of Administration   Here you are.

The **Head of Administration** *lights the two cigarettes and gives one of them to the* **Computer Programmer**.

Computer Programmer   Thank you. How much is that?

Head of Administration   One hundred pesetas.

Computer Programmer   Here you are.

Head of Administration   Thanks.

Computer Programmer   Mind you, this brand is expensive.

Head of Administration   The price has gone up.

Computer Programmer   Yes, I know.

Head of Administration   And now relax, we've got time.

Computer Programmer   Really?

Head of Administration   Yes. Oh, what a pleasure.

Computer Programmer   Yes. So you said we're not the only ones?, that more people from the Company come here to smoke?

Head of Administration   Yes. A few.

Computer Programmer   Who?

Head of Administration   The secret smokers.

Computer Programmer   One or two, apart from us, you mean.

Head of Administration   Maybe more, maybe more.

Computer Programmer   I thought I was the only one cheating the Company. I found it so difficult to lie on the selection tests. Mmm ... I love smoking, I can't help it ... I mean lying ... morally, of course. It was hard.

Head of Administration   My wife and I are getting divorced.

Computer Programmer   Really?

Head of Administration   Yes.

Computer Programmer   That way you'll stop arguing.

Head of Administration   That's why we're getting divorced.

Computer Programmer   Of course.

Pause.

Head of Administration   We don't know what to do with our daughter.

Computer Programmer   Do you want her?

Head of Administration   Yes.

Computer Programmer   I mean, do you want her with you?

Head of Administration   Yes, yes.

Computer Programmer   I mean, custody of her.

Head of Administration   Yes. I know it'll be difficult.

Computer Programmer   Does she want the child?

Head of Administration   I think so.

Computer Programmer   Did you both say so?

Head of Administration   What?

Computer Programmer   To the child.

Head of Administration   What.

Computer Programmer   That you're getting . . .
divorced (what an awful word).

Head of Administration   Yes.

Computer Programmer   So, what did the child say?

Head of Administration   Nothing. She didn't say
anything. Only that she already expected it.

Computer Programmer   I see.

Head of Administration   Pardon?

Computer Programmer   Nothing.

Head of Administration   What do you mean 'nothing'?

Computer Programmer   Nothing, she said nothing.

Head of Administration   Yes, she said nothing.

Computer Programmer   Pardon?

Head of Administration   The child.

Computer Programmer   Oh, I see.

Head of Administration   Yes.

Pause.

Computer Programmer   Do you throw the ash on the
ground?

Pause.

Head of Administration   Pardon?

Pause.

Computer Programmer   My wife and I want to have a
child.

Head of Administration   Congratulations.

Computer Programmer   Thank you.

Head of Administration   It'll change your lives.

Computer Programmer   That's why we want to have
one.

Head of Administration   What do you mean?

Computer Programmer   To change our lives.

Head of Administration   Are you tired of the lives you're
living?

Computer Programmer   Not really.

Head of Administration   What do you mean 'not
really'?

Computer Programmer   Well, yes.

Head of Administration   I see.

Computer Programmer   I mean, no.

Head of Administration   Do you have problems?

Computer Programmer   What? What?

Head of Administration   As a couple.

Computer Programmer   What? No way! Nothing,
nothing at all.

Head of Administration   So, why do you want to
change?

Computer Programmer   Well, I don't know, let's forget
about it, maybe this is not the right time to talk about it,
look, I don't know, we want to have a child and that's all
there is to it, there's no mystery.

Head of Administration   Congratulations.

Computer Programmer   Thank you.

Pause.

Head of Administration   If I wasn't able to have a
smoke from time to time, I don't know what would happen to
me, I like it so much.

Computer Programmer   So do I. It's a pity it's bad.

Head of Administration   Bad?

Computer Programmer   Yes . . . for . . . for your health
. . . isn't it?

Head of Administration   What health?

Pause.

Computer Programmer   How far do you think we are
from the ground?

Head of Administration   Forty-nine storeys, say three
and a half metres each storey, more or less, that's
approximately . . . if I'm not wrong . . . forty-nine times three
fifty three times one hundred and fifty take away three
hundred and forty-seven plus half of forty-nine twenty-four
point five one hundred and forty-seven plus twenty-four
point five one hundred and seventy point five, that's one
hundred and seventy point five metres, approximately.

Computer Programmer   One hundred and seventy
metres!

Head of Administration   And a half.

Computer Programmer   And a half!

Head of Administration   Sorry sorry sorry sorry, I was
wrong. Yes yes yes, because one hundred and forty-seven
plus twenty-four point five is not one hundred and seventy
point five, no, of course, it's one hundred and seventy-one
point five, so it's not one hundred and seventy point five
metres but one hundred and seventy-one point five metres, to
be precise.

Computer Programmer   Well, that doesn't make a
difference.

Head of Administration   No, of course.

Computer Programmer   Is this the highest one in the
city?

Head of Administration   No, come and see.

Computer Programmer   Be careful!!

Head of Administration   It's all right, the railing is safe,
see?

Computer Programmer   Don't! Don't do that!
Everything's so new, so shiny, so . . . Don't you see you could
slip? And everything seems so fragile that . . .

Head of Administration   Look!

Computer Programmer   Ah!

Head of Administration   Only joking. Are you afraid of
heights?

Computer Programmer   No.

Head of Administration   So?

Pause.

Computer Programmer   It's only that you scared me.

Head of Administration   Did I?

Computer Programmer   Yes.

Head of Administration   Why?

Computer Programmer   I don't know. Bec . . .

Head of Administration   No. It's not the highest one.
Look. Come on, come here.

Computer Programmer   Where?

Head of Administration   There, those two, that one and
that one. They're higher. They're new too. Maybe newer
than our one. They weren't there two years ago.

Computer Programmer   Do you think they're higher?

Head of Administration   Yes.

Computer Programmer   I don't know, I don't know.

Pause.

Head of Administration   Not much more, but they're
higher.

Computer Programmer   It must be hard for your daughter.

Head of Administration   My divorce?

Computer Programmer   Yes.

Head of Administration   No.

Computer Programmer   I see.

Pause.

Head of Administration   Maybe.

Computer Programmer   One hundred and seventy metres!

Head of Administration   Yes.

Computer Programmer   Everything seems so small from here. So ridiculous.

Pause.

Head of Administration   Yes.

Pause.

Computer Programmer   What about you?

Head of Administration   What.

Computer Programmer   Has it been hard?

Head of Administration   What.

Computer Programmer   Is it hard?

Head of Administration   No.

Computer Programmer   I see.

Pause.

Head of Administration   A little.

Computer Programmer   I can't imagine it.

Head of Administration   What do you mean.

Computer Programmer   Since I'll never have that kind of problem, the problems as as as as a couple you were talking about, as you say, you know, of course, it's hard for me to understand, all this, you know?, I mean this problem you have, about your your your di . . . your . . . separation, well, me and my wife, we're so happy, you know?, we've always been so happy, we'll never sep . . .

The **Head of Administration** *throws his cigarette over the edge and leans on the railing to watch it fall.*

Head of Administration   One, two, three, four, five, I can't see it any more.

Computer Programmer   What?

Head of Administration   The cigarette. Must have been more than seven seconds.

Computer Programmer   To do what?

Head of Administration   Reach the ground.

Computer Programmer   I see.

Head of Administration   Give me yours.

The **Head of Administration** *takes the* **Computer Programmer**'s *cigarette and throws it over the edge.*

Head of Administration   One, two, three, four, five, six, I can't see it any more.

Computer Programmer   How long would it take for a body to reach the ground?

Head of Administration   That's just what I was thinking.

Computer Programmer   More than seven seconds, surely.

Head of Administration   Probably. What were you saying about your wife?

Computer Programmer   Me? Nothing.

Head of Administration   Perhaps even ten.

Computer Programmer   I said we'll never separate.

Head of Administration   Can you imagine it?

Computer Programmer   What?

Head of Administration   Can you imagine the feeling during those seven or ten seconds?

Computer Programmer   Not really. Can you?

Head of Administration   No.

Computer Programmer   No.

Pause.

Head of Administration   Yes. Yes, I can imagine it.

Computer Programmer   It must be . . .

Head of Administration   Yes, exactly.

Computer Programmer   Shall we go?

Head of Administration   No.

They look at each other. The **Head of Administration** *takes out his little silver case. They light two cigarettes, quickly, in a sort of anxious impulse.*

An explosion, far away. Echo of broken glass, banging, metallic noises, screams one can hardly hear. Almost immediately, a remote but strident sound of sirens getting closer.

They do not move to see what has happened. They are smoking.

Scene 2

Enter, almost pushing each other, the **Blonde Secretary**, *the* **Dark-Haired Secretary**, *the* **Red-Haired Secretary** *and, separated from the others, the* **Brown-Haired Secretary**.

Blonde Secretary   Those stairs are murder, but of course . . .

Dark-Haired Secretary (*to the* **Brown-Haired Secretary**)   Don't you feel well?

Red-Haired Secretary (*to the* **Blonde Secretary**)   What.

Blonde Secretary We don't want to take the lift, of course, in case that poof, the lift-attendant, told anybody, because he's a poof, did you know that?

Dark-Haired Secretary No. Well, it's only ten flights.

Red-Haired Secretary Fourteen, love, fourteen, it's fourteen for me, we're not all that lucky.

Dark-Haired Secretary I don't understand you.

Blonde Secretary By the way, now that we're talking about it, who came up here by lift the other day? It was one of you, because that poof told me, I mean the lift-attendant, that idiot, he asked me, don't you think this lift stinks?, does it?, I said, yes, love, it stinks, it's the disgusting smell of smoke, and I said, well, I can't smell anything, and don't call me love, it pisses me off (especially if it's a poof who calls me that, of course, well, I didn't tell him that, of course, hee, hee, hee), and I said do you think something is burning? (I was pretending I didn't have a clue, of course), and that bloody poof said don't play the fool, miss (he said miss in a nasty way, of course, he said it to avoid calling me love, of course, I told you he's stupid besides being a poof), this stink is the breath of one of your colleagues who's just come down from the roof, you know what I mean, we've made a right cock-up, I thought, I thought we'd agreed that we would go up and down using the emergency stairs, by this I mean that, although I'm really sorry and I don't feel like offending anyone, girls, one of you has betrayed us and doesn't give a shit about our agreements, and that makes me sick, you know, who knows who the fuck the poof has talked to, he might be stupid, but he's not a silly man, or a silly woman, hee, hee, hee, what I mean is that he looked at me as if he knew that I come up here too, and I got nervous, of course, just by thinking he could have been talking with my boss, or my boss's boss, or with your bosses, it made me sick, that's why, having arranged to meet the three of you today, I thought I'd explain the problem straight out and let the traitor or the absent-minded woman, I don't want to accuse anybody, reveal herself, let her at least give an explanation to us and so the four of us can talk about it so that it doesn't happen again, because, girls, if this happens again . . .

Brown-Haired Secretary   It was me.

Pause.

Red-Haired Secretary   I might have known.

Dark-Haired Secretary (*to the* **Blonde Secretary**)   So why did you tell me everything?

Blonde Secretary   Well, I don't know, because you were looking at me, because the look on your face made me think you were listening to me.

Dark-Haired Secretary   Yes, that must have been the reason.

Red-Haired Secretary   I think I'll leave.

Blonde Secretary   You coward.

Red-Haired Secretary   Look, I don't like this at all, I come just to keep you company, I can go without it until after work, I prepare myself mentally, I concentrate, I breathe with my abdomen contracting my diaphragm, I search for my inner self and in half a minute I don't feel like smoking any more.

Blonde Secretary   Oh, come on, love, you're the most addicted one, the thing is you're even more frightened than I am, of course, I'm not surprised, I mean, I can control my boss easily (he drools when he looks at my bottom), and if he gives me a bollocking I don't say anything and then I unbutton my blouse a little bit and get him a coffee I've paid for myself, and the bollocking is forgotten, but of course, I don't know what I'd do with your boss, baby, she's scary, really, she can make you shit yourself, she's always made me shit myself, I mean, she scares the shit out of me.

Dark-Haired Secretary   Listen, what's the problem? We said we would come up here because this is outside the building, so if anybody said anything to us we would remind

them that the order applies only inside the building, and this
is not inside, this is outside.

Red-Haired Secretary   It depends how you look at it.

Dark-Haired Secretary   What do you mean?

Red-Haired Secretary   This isn't *inside* the building, but
it's not exactly *outside* the building either. It's still the
building, in my opinion.

Dark-Haired Secretary   Well, considering how windy
and cold it is, it doesn't look much like any *inside*, to tell you
the truth.

Red-Haired Secretary   Anyway, just in case you've
forgotten, it has nothing to do with the building, love, but
with the Company, it's just the same inside or outside, my
dear, we aren't supposed to be addicted, either inside or
outside, are we?

Blonde Secretary   Excuse me, but I don't find this subject
very interesting.

Brown-Haired Secretary   Will you all shut your
mouths?

Pause.

Blonde Secretary   Our mouths are shut, now.

Pause.

Brown-Haired Secretary   Here you are.

*The **Brown-Haired Secretary** takes out four cigarettes from a
little gold case. She gives one to the **Dark-Haired Secretary**. She
puts one in her mouth. The **Blonde Secretary** takes another one.
She stands there with the fourth cigarette in her hand.*

Brown-Haired Secretary (*to the **Red-Haired Secretary***)
Do you want it or not?

Pause.

Red-Haired Secretary   Yes.

*The **Red-Haired Secretary** grabs the cigarette almost violently.*

Each one lights her cigarette with their own lighter. They smoke.
Silence.

As a matter of fact, I lied to you.

Blonde Secretary   What?

Red-Haired Secretary   My boss can't say anything to me.

Blonde Secretary   Why not?

Red-Haired Secretary   She's an addict, as well.

Blonde Secretary   Really?

Red-Haired Secretary   Last week I found a packet in her briefcase.

Blonde Secretary   A packet! And she managed to get through inspection?

Red-Haired Secretary   They probably didn't notice it.

Blonde Secretary   So what did you do?

Red-Haired Secretary   When she went to the toilet, I took advantage of the situation, I took the packet, which was in an outside pocket of the briefcase, then I opened the packet and dropped it in the main compartment of the case, alongside the files and computer disks. When that bitch returned, she was about to take a piece of paper from the bag and she saw the empty packet and the cigarettes strewn around the inside of the case. Ha, ha, ha. She turned green, the disgusting woman. She lifted her head and began to look around. I'm sure she was thinking: 'I've been found out, I've been found out, someone from the board has found out my secret and has set a trap for me.' And there I was, standing, waiting for her orders, half smiling. Suddenly, she grabbed my arm and said: 'Could you explain your theories on relaxation again?' She wanted to change the subject, poor woman.

Blonde Secretary   But she scares you.

Red-Haired Secretary   Of course. But I know her secrets.

Blonde Secretary   Well, just one.

Dark-Haired Secretary (*to the* **Blonde Secretary**) Your boss has come up here more than once. At least once. The other day.

Blonde Secretary   How do you know?

Dark-Haired Secretary   That bloke told me, the one who works with computers.

Blonde Secretary   The Programmer?

Dark-Haired Secretary   Yes. I met him once, he had just come down from here and he was entering the floor where he works through the emergency door. He was suffering so much, poor guy. He told me he had been looking at the scenery with your boss, that they had had a bet about the height of some building or other . . . He turned bright red with embarrassment. He noticed I was holding back my laughter. He noticed I knew he was lying. I think he also noticed that I find him very attractive.

Blonde Secretary   My boss is completely obsessed with the height of everything, maybe that Programmer wasn't lying. By the way, I find that guy very attractive, as well.

Red-Haired Secretary   If he got nervous he was lying. And I don't find him attractive.

Dark-Haired Secretary   He got really nervous.

Blonde Secretary   As a matter of fact, my boss is obsessed about loads of things.

Red-Haired Secretary   Well. Like everybody else.

Pause.

Blonde Secretary   He gave me a dress as a birthday present. My boss, I mean.

Pause.

Red-Haired Secretary   I don't know who told me, but he's getting divorced.

Blonde Secretary   Made of pure silk.

Brown-Haired Secretary   I'd stay here for an hour.

Dark-Haired Secretary   It's too cold.

Brown-Haired Secretary   No. I like it.

Red-Haired Secretary   God, it must be really expensive.

Blonde Secretary   It is. Pure silk, do you hear?, from top to bottom, with little silver buttons.

Red-Haired Secretary   Who didn't understand me when I said that some people are lucky?

Brown-Haired Secretary   I think somebody's coming.

Sudden silence. Tension.

No. Nobody's coming.

Pause. They continue smoking.

Blonde Secretary   Well, the truth is I've got a problem with this dress, a huge, horrible problem, perhaps you could help me, I'd be very very grateful if you could give me any ideas, any solutions. You see, the problem is I have no shoes. And no bag, no bag. I mean, I haven't found any shoes or bag to match the dress, it's a green dress, a very strange green, an impossible green. Last Saturday I looked in all the shoeshops in town, all the shopping centres, all the shops, even the most expensive ones, even the most luxurious ones, I'd have paid anything, because I've got enough money for shoes and bags, and I don't mind spending it because I can and I like it and I can afford it and it's a special occasion, but nothing at all, there were only black shoes and black bags, and you know very well, girls, how much I hate black, I can't stand it, I find it horrible, it's astonishing how unsexy it is for shoes and bags, so I don't know what to do, the dress is hanging in the wardrobe and there's nothing I can do about the shoes and the bag, the shoes and the bag I can't find, and the thing is I like that dress, don't I?, it's quite pretty, it is, it goes down to here, maybe even higher, to here, yes, to here, well, maybe not so much, well, I don't know, oh, and it's made of real silk, it is, and it hardly has any seams, it's made by a very famous designer, oh yes, very very famous, I can't remember his name now, but everybody knows him, his designs are always very expensive and have very strange colours, actually, the colour is very beautiful, it is, but it doesn't match anything, because I didn't find the shoes, or the bag, not even a jacket or a coat, or anything that matches it to wear over it, so I'm desperate and I don't know what to do with the dress. I might give it back to him.

Red-Haired Secretary   Give it to me.

Pause.

Blonde Secretary   You don't give presents away.

Dark-Haired Secretary   Or give them back, either.

Blonde Secretary   Yes.

Dark-Haired Secretary   No.

Blonde Secretary   Yes, love, yes, they can change it for another one. They've got to change it for another one if it doesn't fit you or you don't like it.

Red-Haired Secretary   But you said you loved it.

Blonde Secretary   You're wrong, Señora, excuse me, but I didn't say I loved it, I said it wasn't bad.

Red-Haired Secretary   Come on, girl, shut your mouth, you're giving me a headache.

Dark-Haired Secretary (*to the* **Brown-Haired Secretary**)   What are you doing? What are you thinking about? Why are you so quiet? Don't you have vertigo? What are you looking at?

Brown-Haired Secretary   I'm just looking.

Dark-Haired Secretary   What at?

Brown-Haired Secretary   Nothing. The street. The people.

Red-Haired Secretary   You must have very good eyesight.

Brown-Haired Secretary   There's a perfectly still woman who's looking at somebody from the window of a house. It's an old, small, strange house. The woman was looking at somebody who was in the street.

Red-Haired Secretary   Oh, how interesting.

Brown-Haired Secretary   She was crying. She must feel miserable. It's probably her own fault. She's a married woman. She chose by inertia a sort of life she's not happy with. She feels obliged to love the man she chose and, in fact, she doesn't love him. I'm sure it's her fault. She doesn't know what's forcing her, but she feels forced. She was looking through the window with misty eyes. Look at her. She's coming back. She's grabbed the curtains. Yes. She's looking at someone in the street. Who is it? Oh yes. A man. Look at him, that one. He's blond, strong, tall. She opens her eyes. What's she doing now? She draws the curtains back with a solemn, elegant movement. The man on the street stops walking. He feels observed. She opens the window. She leans out of the window. The man looks at her. The woman looks at the man. They remain still, looking at each other. How strange. Now she draws herself upright, turns, goes in, closes the window, draws the curtains. He crosses the street, almost running, where's he going? Yes, yes, he's entering the house, I knew it. I'm sure they don't know each other. I'm sure he'll climb the stairs, anxious, panting, and knock at her door. She'll open it. I'm sure that, without a word, they'll make love like animals.

Blonde Secretary   What a thing to say.

Red-Haired Secretary (*to the* **Blonde Secretary**)   She's making it up.

Blonde Secretary   Of course, no doubt about it!

Red-Haired Secretary   I've always thought she's got big problems, that girl.

Blonde Secretary   Yes, yes, I think so too and as long as they don't affect us, you know, I'm all right, but when these problems affect us, like this one with the lift, I don't take it lying down, no way.

Brown-Haired Secretary   Look, look. He's already in. They're clutching each other. They're taking their clothes off. I knew it. Just like wild beasts.

Dark-Haired Secretary   That's not true. You can't see anything from here.

Brown-Haired Secretary   Yes you can.

Dark-Haired Secretary   Let me see.

The **Dark-Haired Secretary** *goes towards the railing, makes a wrong move and slips. The* **Blonde Secretary** *and the* **Red-Haired Secretary** *become frightened and scream hysterically. The* **Brown-Haired Secretary** *grabs the arm of the* **Dark-Haired Secretary***, who has almost half her body hanging over the edge, and pulls her back. Tension.*

Brown-Haired Secretary   Why did you do that?

Dark-Haired Secretary   I didn't do anything.

Brown-Haired Secretary   Why did you do it?

Dark-Haired Secretary   I slipped.

Blonde Secretary   You stupid woman, I don't like that kind of joke. Oh, I've got my heart in my mouth!

Red-Haired Secretary (*to the* **Blonde Secretary**) Everything she does is to attract people's attention, I can't stand her, I can't stand her!

Blonde Secretary   Oh! Oh! Ah!

Red-Haired Secretary   And now don't you get hysterical, all right?, don't get hysterical, breathe, concentrate, relax, but don't get hysterical, do you hear me?, I said don't get hysterical!!!

Blonde Secretary   Shut up, you're just a pain in the neck!

The **Blonde Secretary** *slaps the* **Red-Haired Secretary**. *The* **Dark-Haired Secretary** *bursts into tears.*

Red-Haired Secretary   We must go back.

The **Red-Haired Secretary** *exits.*

Blonde Secretary (*to the* **Dark-Haired Secretary**)   Now she'll be angry with me, and it's all your fault.

The **Blonde Secretary** *exits.*

Brown-Haired Secretary   You scared me as well.

Dark-Haired Secretary   What's wrong with you all?

Exit the **Brown-Haired Secretary**. *The* **Dark-Haired Secretary** *is left alone, crying in silence. Suddenly, she goes towards the railing and looks down.*

Dark-Haired Secretary   I can't see them.

Violent gust of wind.

Scene 3

The **Local Messenger**, *alone.*

He goes near the railing. He looks down. He shouts.

Local Messenger   Americaaaaaaaaa!!!

Echo.

He takes out a pocket Digital Compact Cassette Player. He places a tape in it, and puts on the headphones. He sings and dances, intermittently repeating the song he's listening to through the headphones, really loudly. He unbuttons his fly, puts his hand inside, gropes around and takes out a cigarette, wrapped in foil. He lights it.

A helicopter flies above the building, very near to the roof. The **Local Messenger** *hears the noise. Wind. He removes his headphones. He looks upwards. The helicopter moves away.*

Some day, one of those blasted machines will crash into a building.

He puts his headphones back on. Instantaneously, a loud noise is heard nearby. Explosion. Yellowish and reddish lights. Noise of broken glass. He goes up to the railing, removes his headphones.

Fuck, fuck, fuck, fuck!

He doesn't know what to do. He walks to and fro. He puts his cigarette out. He almost exits, but then comes back. He leans on the railing and looks out. Smoke. Confusion. Sirens. Cries for help.

Fuck, I feel sick, I feel sick . . .

He vomits over the edge, leaning on the railing. He draws himself up. He sits on the floor, exhausted. He lights another cigarette. The sky is red.

Enter the **Female Managing Director**. *The* **Local Messenger** *puts his cigarette out quickly and throws it over the edge.*

Female Managing Director   Who are you?

Local Messenger   One of the messengers.

Female Managing Director   With our Company?

Local Messenger   Yes.

Female Managing Director   What happened?

Local Messenger   I don't know, I don't know anything, I think it was a helicopter. An accident.

Female Managing Director   What were you doing here?

Local Messenger   No . . . nothing, I came . . . to watch the helicopters . . .

Female Managing Director   Go immediately unless you want me to report you at the next Board Meeting.

Local Messenger   Yes, madam.

He is about to leave. He stops.

Did you see, how terrible?

Female Managing Director   Yes, very, very terrible. Go, they'll probably want to evacuate the building. I'll be down in a moment.

Exit the **Local Messenger**.

The **Female Managing Director** *looks everywhere, goes up to the access door to the roof to make sure nobody is coming. She takes out a cigarette from a little grey case she had in her hand. She lights it. She smokes with pleasure. She goes near the railing and looks towards the place where the accident has happened.*

Female Managing Director   How beautiful.

Scene 4

Enter the **Head of Administration** *and the* **Computer Programmer**. *They walk towards the railing. They look at each other. The* **Computer Programmer** *embraces the* **Head of Administration**. *They separate. They look at each other. The* **Head of Administration** *nods. The* **Computer Programmer** *throws himself over the edge. A scream. Echo. The* **Head of Administration** *coldly watches him fall.*

Head of Administration   Eight seconds. Approximately.

He lights a cigarette.

Scene 5

Enter the **Blonde Secretary**.

Blonde Secretary   This is the first time I've come up here. Oh, how beautiful!

Pause.

Do you hear me?

Pause.

Can I ask you a question?

Pause.

Enter the **Head of Administration**.

Blonde Secretary   Why are you looking at me like that?

Head of Administration   What question?

Blonde Secretary   Mmmm . . . do you smoke?

Head of Administration   No.

Blonde Secretary   Me neither.

Head of Administration   Nobody smokes here, don't you remember?

Blonde Secretary   Yes, of course, sorry, I don't know why I thought . . .

Pause.

Head of Administration   Was that the question you wanted to ask me?

Blonde Secretary   Well, no.

Head of Administration   I'm listening.

Blonde Secretary   I don't know if I have the courage . . . But, since we're here . . . outside the office . . . Well, yes: why did you do it?

Head of Administration   What?

Blonde Secretary   The dress.

Head of Administration   I can't answer.

Blonde Secretary   Why?

Head of Administration   Personal reasons.

Blonde Secretary   Sorry, but I don't understand you.

Head of Administration   There's no reason why you should understand me.

Blonde Secretary   And why not? What a thing to say, look, now I'll be frank with you, a present . . . a present is . . . a present means . . . it means, between the person who gives it and the person who receives it, the woman who receives it, I mean when a person gives a present to someone else, and even worse, or better, when the gift is a personal thing like a dress or an intimate thing or such a personal thing as a bra or a pair of knickers or garters or, for instance, a dress or even lipstick or a bottle of perfume or such a personal and intimate thing as a dress, well, what I mean is, when you do that, generally, I mean the most normal and natural and very normal thing in the world is that him and me, I mean between the one spending the money and me receiving the gift, well, the most natural thing is that, between them or him and me, there is, how can I put it, oh, now I don't know how to say it, well, I believe there has to be a relationship a little more, a little bit more, how could I put it, let's see, closer, closer, I mean more like this, yeah?, a lot more like this than the relationship there can be between a secretary, however efficient and intelligent she is, and her so-and-so, her boss, don't you think so?, I mean . . .

Head of Administration   All right.

Blonde Secretary   Ah.

Pause.

Head of Administration   You are so stupid.

Pause.

Blonde Secretary   Oh.

Head of Administration   So stupid, so obtuse, so limited, so pathetic that you move me to pity.

Blonde Secretary   Oh. I don't know what to say.

Head of Administration   Shut up, then.

Blonde Secretary   Oh.

The **Head of Administration** *takes out a cigarette and smokes it.*

Blonde Secretary   Ooh!!

Head of Administration   What's wrong with you?

Blonde Secretary   You smoke!!

Head of Administration   Will you stop pretending, please?, it's quite disgusting.

Blonde Secretary   But you told me . . .

Head of Administration   Not only is this not the first time you've been up here but, besides, nicotine flows from your ears, your nose, your mouth, your eyes and all the rest of the orifices in your body, if you'll pardon the expression. But I didn't tell you to come up here to accuse you of being addicted, as you can see I'm addicted as well, it wasn't to ask you for anything either . . . anything special, you understand what I mean, don't you?, but, I told you to come up here to talk very seriously about a regrettable error you committed.

Blonde Secretary   What error?

Head of Administration   Telling your colleagues that I gave you that dress.

Blonde Secretary   Is that a regrettable error?

Head of Administration   Yes it is, there's no doubt about that.

Blonde Secretary   And that makes me stupid?

Head of Administration   No, not because of that. You're stupid in general.

Blonde Secretary   And limited and pathetic?

Head of Administration   In general, as well. You were, you are and you'll always be.

Blonde Secretary   Oh.

Head of Administration   Stop crying, please.

Blonde Secretary   The thing is I don't understand anything . . . and whenever I don't understand anything I get nervous and then . . . I feel like crying.

Head of Administration   What is it that you don't understand?

Blonde Secretary   I can't understand why saying that you were so kind and so charming to give me a dress, why that has to be an error, and a regrettable one at that.

Head of Administration   Because now my colleagues, and this is all your fault, they feel obliged to do the same. Otherwise, their secretaries have threatened not to do their work properly.

Blonde Secretary   Hee, hee, hee . . .

Head of Administration   Obviously, they're not very happy about that, everybody despises me, and somebody has even considered punishing me.

Blonde Secretary   . . . hee, hee, hee . . .

Head of Administration   Have you ever thought what happens when a body falls over the edge and hits the ground from a height of over one hundred metres?

Blonde Secretary   . . . hee, hee . . . No.

Head of Administration   I have. The body explodes.

Blonde Secretary   All right, I'll shut up, I'll shut up.

Pause.

It explodes?

Head of Administration   Yes.

Blonde Secretary   Like that helicopter did yesterday?

Head of Administration   Worse, much worse, it explodes inside.

Blonde Secretary   That's revolting, isn't it?

Head of Administration   You are so stupid.

Blonde Secretary   Are you sure you don't want anything . . . from me?

Head of Administration   You're stupid but beautiful. However, you must know you'll never get anything from me. Ever.

Blonde Secretary   You're wrong. Oh, sorry. At least I got a dress.

Head of Administration   Well . . . yes.

Blonde Secretary   Personal reasons, you said?

Head of Administration   Yes.

Blonde Secretary   It was a present for your wife, wasn't it?

Pause.

Or, more precisely . . . ex-wife.

Pause.

Head of Administration   Yes.

Pause.

Blonde Secretary   You look pale.

Head of Administration   It's the cold.

Blonde Secretary   Are you scared of heights?

Head of Administration   What about you?

Blonde Secretary   I'm not.

Head of Administration   Me neither.

Blonde Secretary   That's not true.

Head of Administration   Yes it is.

Blonde Secretary   You look really pale, anyway.

Head of Administration   I feel OK.

Blonde Secretary   Me too.

Head of Administration   Did I upset you with those things I said?

Pause.

Blonde Secretary   What did you say?

Pause.

Head of Administration   Nothing.

Blonde Secretary   I see.

Head of Administration   Am I really pale?

Blonde Secretary   Yes.

Head of Administration   I didn't sleep very well, last night. I had a nightmare: one of the computer programmers threw himself over this very railing, before my very eyes.

Blonde Secretary   The one who's been coming up to smoke with you all week long?

Head of Administration   So, you're also spying on us?

Blonde Secretary   Me? No, I don't know, somebody must have told me something, I don't know, I don't know anything, oh, listen, I'm not a spy, am I?, why are you always suspicious of me? So, what else happened in your dream?

Head of Administration   Nothing else.

Blonde Secretary   And his body, did it explode?

Head of Administration   Yes.

Blonde Secretary   That's revolting, isn't it?

Head of Administration   No, I didn't see it.

Blonde Secretary   And what's that got to do with your wife? I mean we were talking about her, weren't we?

Head of Administration   I don't remember.

Pause.

Let's go down.

Blonde Secretary   No.

Pause.

Head of Administration   What did you say?

Blonde Secretary   Me? Nothing.

Head of Administration   Don't stay too long, we've got work to do.

The **Head of Administration** *turns to leave.*

Blonde Secretary   Wait.

The **Blonde Secretary** *goes towards him, puts her hand in his pocket, takes out a cigarette and a lighter. She lights the cigarette and puts the lighter back in his pocket.*

Thank you. You can go now. I'll come down at once. When I finish my cigarette. You will let me, won't you? And you won't tell anybody, will you? Thank you. Oh, if you still feel awful, take a pill, I've got some in my bag, it's hanging on my chair, take one, oh, by the way, you'd better not use the lift, the assistant has got a very good sense of smell.

Head of Administration   Me too.

Blonde Secretary   But he's a big mouth, and you're not.

Head of Administration   No.

Exit the **Head of Administration**. *The* **Blonde Secretary** *goes to the railing. She leans on it. She looks over the edge. She smokes. She smiles. All at once, she bursts out laughing. After a moment she suddenly stops laughing.*

Blonde Secretary   Oh, now I don't know what I was laughing about.

She puts the cigarette out and runs off.

Scene 6

Enter the **Dark-Haired Secretary**, *the* **Red-Haired Secretary** *and the* **Local Messenger**.

Dark-Haired Secretary   These things sometimes happen.

Local Messenger   As if it were my fault.

Dark-Haired Secretary   But why?

Local Messenger   I've already told you. I thought: some day, one of those blasted machines will crash into a building and, you know what, it didn't happen some day, but at that very moment, just a second after I'd thought about it.

Dark-Haired Secretary   It was sheer coincidence.

Red-Haired Secretary   I don't believe in coincidences.

Pause.

Dark-Haired Secretary   Don't you?

Red-Haired Secretary   No.

Dark-Haired Secretary   So what do you believe in?

Red-Haired Secretary   Shall I explain?

Local Messenger   Explain what?

Red-Haired Secretary   My theory.

Dark-Haired Secretary   Oh, no.

Red-Haired Secretary   My theory about the helicopter accident.

Local Messenger   All right, yes, but if you're going to scare me . . .

Red-Haired Secretary   Sit down.

Dark-Haired Secretary   Where?

Red-Haired Secretary   On the ground. It's clean.

Dark-Haired Secretary   Listen, what if we aren't interested in your theory?

Red-Haired Secretary   I'll explain it to you anyway.

Dark-Haired Secretary   I'm leaving.

Local Messenger   I'm interested in it.

Dark-Haired Secretary   Of course, you can't miss it, you're probably the hero of the story, aren't you?

Red-Haired Secretary   Obviously.

Pause. The **Red-Haired Secretary** *stares at the* **Dark-Haired Secretary**.

Didn't you say you were leaving?

Dark-Haired Secretary   Now I don't want to.

Red-Haired Secretary   I'm going to talk whether you like it or not.

The **Dark-Haired Secretary** *sits down on the ground. The* **Local Messenger** *does the same.*

Red-Haired Secretary   Are you ready? Well, here goes.

The **Computer Programmer** *comes on stage. He has an unlit cigarette in his mouth. He sees the others and quickly removes the cigarette from his mouth.*

Computer Programmer   Sorry.

Pause.

Good morning.

Red-Haired Secretary   No, no, you're not disturbing us. And don't worry, we've known about your habit for many days, don't worry, come on, don't worry, would you like to sit down here with us?, I was about to explain a quite interesting theory about the telekinetic power of our minds.

Local Messenger   Tele what? Uh, oh, and do I have it?

Dark-Haired Secretary   I doubt it . . .

Computer Programmer   No, no, thank you very much . . . but I was looking for . . .

Red-Haired Secretary   Oh yes, the Head of Administration, right? Yes, we already know you've been coming up here all week long non-stop, don't worry, we know it all, come on, and you needn't worry, we'll keep as quiet as mice.

Computer Programmer   And do you know where he is?

Red-Haired Secretary   He went down to the thirty-fifth floor, to my boss's office. They've been having meetings all the time, lately, do you know why?

Computer Programmer   No.

Red-Haired Secretary   Well, are you staying?

Computer Programmer   No.

Red-Haired Secretary   Goodbye, then.

The **Computer Programmer** *leaves.*

Red-Haired Secretary   I can't stand that bloke.

Local Messenger   What about your theory?

Dark-Haired Secretary   I want to have a smoke.

Local Messenger   Me too.

Dark-Haired Secretary   Have you got any fags?

Local Messenger   Yes.

The **Local Messenger** *takes out two cigarettes from an inside pocket of his trousers. He lights them and gives one of them to the* **Dark-Haired Secretary**.

Red-Haired Secretary   Well, are you listening to me or not?

The **Computer Programmer** *comes on again*.

Computer Programmer   The thing is I wasn't really looking for the Head of Administration, I came to . . .

Red-Haired Secretary   To have a smoke.

Computer Programmer   Oh, no, no . . . Well . . . yes . . . but . . . but also to breathe . . . I can't stand air-conditioning . . . I think I'm allergic to air-conditioning, especially the one in our offices . . . which is scented air-conditioning, I must be allergic to the scent rather than to the air . . . it's a forest scent, a natural scent, I think.

Red-Haired Secretary   Listen, could you shut up? Can't you see you're interrupting us?

The **Dark-Haired Secretary** *stands up*.

Red-Haired Secretary   And now why are you standing up?

Dark-Haired Secretary   My legs are hurting.

Local Messenger (*to the* **Computer Programmer**)   Do you want a light?

Computer Programmer   No, I've got one, thank you.

Red-Haired Secretary   Are you listening to me or what?

Computer Programmer   Go ahead, go ahead, I don't want to interrupt you. I'll go to a corner.

Red-Haired Secretary (*to the* **Dark-Haired Secretary**) You, sit down.

Dark-Haired Secretary   What if I don't want to?

Red-Haired Secretary   Go away.

The **Dark-Haired Secretary** *sits down, continuing to look at the* **Computer Programmer**, *who has gone to a corner, is leaning on the railing and has started smoking.*

Red-Haired Secretary   Well, my theory goes like this . . .

All of a sudden, the **Female Managing Director** *enters.*

Female Managing Director   Has anybody seen the Head of Administration?

The **Computer Programmer**, *the* **Dark-Haired Secretary** *and the* **Local Messenger** *put their cigarettes out quickly and throw them away. The* **Local Messenger**, *when he sees the* **Female Managing Director**, *hides behind the* **Dark-Haired Secretary**.

Computer Programmer   No, he's not here.

Female Managing Director   I can see, I'm not blind.

Red-Haired Secretary   But he was in his office a moment ago.

Female Managing Director   What are you doing here?

Red-Haired Secretary   I came for a breath of fresh air, I'm slightly allergic to the natural forest scented air-conditioning and, since you were having another one of those meetings where you don't need me at all, well, I thought I could . . .

Female Managing Director   All right, all right. So you haven't seen him. He told me he was going to the toilet for a second. But it's been twenty minutes and he's not back.

Dark-Haired Secretary   He might be constipated.

Female Managing Director Who was that?

Dark-Haired Secretary Me.

Female Managing Director Who are you?

Dark-Haired Secretary The secretary of the Head of Personnel Recruitment.

Female Managing Director With our Company?

Dark-Haired Secretary Yes.

Female Managing Director Oh. I didn't know you. Nice to meet you. I'm leaving. (*To the* **Red-Haired Secretary**.) And I want *you* in the office in five minutes. Goodbye.

The **Female Managing Director** *exits. Immediately, the* **Computer Programmer**, *the* **Dark-Haired Secretary** *and the* **Local Messenger** *each light a cigarette.*

Local Messenger What a woman, eh?

Red-Haired Secretary She's not a woman, she's a monster, a machine. And now, my theory.

Dark-Haired Secretary (*to the* **Computer Programmer**) Aren't you afraid of looking down?

Red-Haired Secretary Shut uuuup!!!

Pause.

Well. All right. Here goes. My theory goes like this: we all have a disproportionate energy in here, in our heads, more precisely in our brains. And we don't know how to control it, how to measure it, we can't manipulate it how we want. Lots of times, or sometimes, it depends on the person, a hidden, shameful, maybe unconscious desire has such a mental strength, such an energetic, pure, incommensurable force, such a metaphysical force (give me a fag, now that I'm warming up . . . thanks), such a force that this energy, which has been becoming concentrated and condensed, emerges from our bodies to avoid causing an internal explosion and causes strange phenomena such as accidents, tragedies or the deaths of people we hate.

Local Messenger   So you mean I was to blame for . . . But I didn't hate anybody . . . I didn't even know who was flying the helicopter . . . I didn't know any of the one hundred and thirty-seven dead people either . . . Maybe I knew them but just by sight, from having seen them in the street. Besides, I don't want to hurt anybody, I've never even killed a fly.

Red-Haired Secretary   That's what you think.

Dark-Haired Secretary (*to the* **Computer Programmer**)   Aren't you afraid of looking down?

Computer Programmer   What did you say?

Dark-Haired Secretary   Aren't you afraid of leaning on the railing, like this?

Red-Haired Secretary   Listen, love, are you trying to put me off or what?

Dark-Haired Secretary   What? Oh, no, sorry, I'm just not convinced by your theory.

The **Red-Haired Secretary** *throws her cigarette to the ground, near the* **Dark-Haired Secretary** *and crushes it with her foot. The* **Dark-Haired Secretary** *stands up and goes towards the* **Computer Programmer**.

Dark-Haired Secretary   Aren't you afraid of heights?

Computer Programmer   A little bit. That's precisely why I'm standing here, to fight against it. To lose my fear.

Dark-Haired Secretary   The other day I nearly fell.

Red-Haired Secretary (*to the* **Local Messenger**)   She wants to score with him.

Local Messenger   So what.

Dark-Haired Secretary   Right here. I slipped, I made a wrong move. I was scared. This railing is not very safe.

Computer Programmer   It's very safe.

Red-Haired Secretary (*to the* **Local Messenger**)   I noticed it immediately. Look at her, look at her, what eyes, she's devouring him with her eyes, the t . . .

Local Messenger   I'm leaving.

Red-Haired Secretary   Wait, come on, wait. I hadn't finished.

Local Messenger   I've got work to do, you know?

Red-Haired Secretary   Do I scare you or what?

Local Messenger   Yes.

Computer Programmer   Does it scare you?

Dark-Haired Secretary   Yes.

Computer Programmer   You've got to trust me. Come here.

Red-Haired Secretary   Oh, oh, they're almost on top of each other!

Local Messenger   Yes, you do scare me, you really scare me because because because because I think you're fucking attractive and I'd like to screw you, that's it, now I've told you! Phew, now I've got that off my mind, I can leave.

Red-Haired Secretary   Don't leave me alone.

Computer Programmer   See? You're not afraid any more, are you?

Dark-Haired Secretary   No, because you're holding me.

Local Messenger   Do you want to come out with me tonight?

Red-Haired Secretary   Listen, kid, will you shut up? I can't hear what they're saying.

Local Messenger   Why the hell do you care?

Computer Programmer   Your colleague is a bit special.

Dark-Haired Secretary   Who, her?

Computer Programmer   Yes.

Dark-Haired Secretary   She's not special at all. She's just hysterical.

Local Messenger   If you don't come out with me tonight, I'm leaving.

Red-Haired Secretary   Shh.

Dark-Haired Secretary   Would you like to come out with me tonight?

Computer Programmer   What? To do what?

Dark-Haired Secretary   I don't know. To talk. To have dinner. To . . .

Computer Programmer   Can my wife come as well?

Dark-Haired Secretary   No.

Computer Programmer   I'm not coming, then.

Red-Haired Secretary   Bitch.

Local Messenger   You're crazy.

Dark-Haired Secretary   I'd like to throw myself over the edge right now.

Computer Programmer   Why?

Dark-Haired Secretary   Because of the embarrassment I'm feeling. You must think I'm a . . .

Red-Haired Secretary   . . . a bitch. She is.

Local Messenger   Well, it's your loss.

The **Local Messenger** *spits on the ground, near the feet of the* **Red-Haired Secretary**, *throws his cigarette over the edge and exits.*

Computer Programmer (*to the* **Red-Haired Secretary**)   If you want to, you can come closer, to hear better.

Red-Haired Secretary   Pardon? Are you talking to me? No, I was just going . . .

Dark-Haired Secretary   What? You lousy liar, you repulsive, jealous fucking hole, you damn jealous bitch, you were going? you lying cow, you couldn't take your eyes off us, you couldn't take your eyes off him and you said you can't stand him, she said I can't stand that bloke and now you can't take your eyes off him, you shit-sucking, esoteric cow, I wish a gust of wind would throw you over the edge and splatter you on the ground and make you explode, all of you, in the fall, all of you a great explosion, all of you a botch of crushed limbs, you uncouth liar, you dull-witted, uncultured repulsive bitch!!

The **Dark-Haired Secretary** *runs off.*

Red-Haired Secretary (*to the* **Computer Programmer**)   Can you give me a fag?

Computer Programmer   I only have this one.

Red-Haired Secretary   Can I have a puff?

Computer Programmer   No. I'm a bit fussy.

Red-Haired Secretary   I can't stand you.

Computer Programmer   I know.

Red-Haired Secretary   Do you want me to explain my theories?

The **Computer Programmer** *throws his cigarette over the edge and leaves. The* **Red-Haired Secretary** *leans on the railing and looks at the sky.*

Strange things happen when people hate each other.

Suddenly, a strong gust of wind blows across the roof. The **Red-Haired Secretary** *gets scared. She has to cling to the railing with all her strength to avoid falling over.*

Oh! Help! I don't want to fall, I don't want to fall! Oh my God, my God, help me, merciful God!

Scene 7

Enter the **Head of Administration**, *the* **Brown-Haired Secretary** *and the* **Female Managing Director**.

Female Managing Director   Nobody will hear us here.

Brown-Haired Secretary   I'm not sure. There's been more movement here, lately, than in the lifts.

The **Head of Administration** *takes out a packet of cigarettes.*

Head of Administration   Do you want one?

Female Managing Director   What? We didn't come up here to . . . to smoke. Besides, I don't smoke, she doesn't either, only *you* fail to observe the rules, and I won't say anything because we're friends, you know, we didn't come up here to relax . . .

Head of Administration   But . . .

Female Managing Director   We came up here to work.

Brown-Haired Secretary   I do smoke.

Female Managing Director   Oh.

Pause.

Smoking doesn't distract you?

Brown-Haired Secretary   Not at all.

Female Managing Director   In that case, you can smoke.

Head of Administration   What about me?

Female Managing Director   Do what you like, it's up to you.

Head of Administration   Here.

Brown-Haired Secretary   Thank you.

Head of Administration   You can pay for it later, don't worry.

Brown-Haired Secretary   Thank you.

The **Head of Administration** *and the* **Brown-Haired Secretary** *light their cigarettes.*

Female Managing Director   Have you finished? All right. I guess you're wondering why we've summoned you here.

Brown-Haired Secretary   Yes.

Female Managing Director   I guess you want an explanation.

Brown-Haired Secretary   I feel a bit uncomfortable.

Head of Administration   No wonder.

The **Female Managing Director** *looks at the* **Head of Administration** *angrily. Pause.*

Female Managing Director   Will you let me continue? Thank you. Well. You're here with us in your capacity as secretary.

Brown-Haired Secretary   Well, yes, but I can't understand why . . .

Female Managing Director   You don't need to understand anything, for the moment. I know you'll find our proposals strange. Well, it's about . . . I don't know how to explain it now, I'm a little nervous too. You explain it to her.

Head of Administration   Me?

Female Managing Director   Yes. Start from the beginning, for instance. Or better with her, start with her, explain why we chose her.

Head of Administration   She's intelligent enough. She must have guessed why.

Brown-Haired Secretary   I can't guess anything and I don't know what you're talking about.

Head of Administration   We chose you by a process of elimination, by a simple process of elimination. The range of secretaries in our company is quite limited, being clever as you are, you must have noticed that. Their abilities don't

exactly stand out. Mine is not much more than mentally
retarded. Besides, she's dishonest, rude, uncultured, dirty,
badly dressed, her nails are too long and she wants to get me
into bed like a common prostitute to get promoted, how
naïve, poor thing, I don't know what post she could fill,
considering her non-existent mental capacity. By the way,
I've always been curious to know how she managed to pass
the Basic Skills Test, probably by sleeping with the Head of
Personnel Recruitment, we should investigate these
irregularities thoroughly and you should expose the matter
at the next Board Meeting.

Female Managing Director   No need. I already have at
the last one, just yesterday. He's just been dismissed, two
hours ago. I met him in the toilets. He was throwing up.

Head of Administration   Poor thing.

Female Managing Director   Poor thing? Now you feel
sorry for him?

Head of Administration   I've always thought he was a
good man, at heart.

Female Managing Director   Well, enough of that.

Head of Administration   What were we talking about?

Brown-Haired Secretary   About the . . . the inefficiency
of your secretary.

Head of Administration   Oh, yes. By the way, do you
know who she is?

Brown-Haired Secretary   Yes. The dark-haired one.

Head of Administration   No. She's blonde.

Brown-Haired Secretary   No, she's dark-haired. Dyed
blonde.

Female Managing Director   Ha ha ha.

Head of Administration   Yes, so . . . that's it. We need
an efficient and intelligent secretary. Mine is, therefore,
obviously, ruled out.

Female Managing Director   There's mine.

Brown-Haired Secretary   The idiot.

Female Managing Director   Pardon?

Brown-Haired Secretary   The red-haired one.

Female Managing Director   Yes.

Brown-Haired Secretary   We call her the idiot.

Female Managing Director   I see. I didn't know.

Brown-Haired Secretary   She's dark-haired as well

Female Managing Director   You know everything.

Brown-Haired Secretary   No I don't.

Female Managing Director   Well, what's wrong with mine, apart from the fact that you consider her stupid, is that she suffers from serious problems . . . how can I put it? . . . psychological problems, as it were.

Brown-Haired Secretary   Oh, really?

Female Managing Director   Yes. She confuses competitivity with war and dialogue with argument. Besides . . . now I know I'm being a bit indiscreet, nobody knows about it, I think, only me, she confessed it to me a few days ago . . . she's also a believer.

Head of Administration   Oh. You hadn't told me about that.

Female Managing Director   Actually, I've never thought she was inefficient, on the contrary, she's clever and works fast, a little bit too nervous but efficient, reliable and very dynamic. The problems come when she relaxes and gets carried away by her fantasies (she calls them theories).

Brown-Haired Secretary   I don't understand.

Female Managing Director   The problems arise when she's got to think on her own. When the work is not mechanical but thoughtful. I don't know if I'm making myself clear. Secretaries, in my opinion, must know how to

think for themselves, as well. They must be able to assess
their bosses' state of mind and behave accordingly. If their
heads are full of acquired, impersonal, esoteric and ritual
theories, if they believe in predestination and in superior
entities that guide us and control us and manipulate us as
they wish, they don't do anything to try to change the course
of events and they become what she is: a person who's crazy
about the established order, inflexible and unable to change
anything to open up new horizons which are out of the
ordinary and boring work of the traditonal secretary, in
other words, she becomes reactionary, a pure conservative. I
need, we need something different. A brain, some sensitivity,
some character, a person. Not a machine that's stupidified
by the weight of established order and tradition.

Brown-Haired Secretary   I don't understand what
you're getting at.

Female Managing Director   Yes, you do. You've been
suspecting it all the time and don't dare ask. I want, we want
to break off from the Company and create a new company
with no overriding desire for profit-making, just to enjoy it,
for pleasure, for the pleasure of knowing we are the heroes of
an adventure without depending on an impersonal,
devouring monster, we want a small company, drawn to our
own measurements, but intelligent, with intelligent people,
to do an intelligent job, with no other ambition than being
happy, without being accountable to anybody, without
being a lowly and depersonalized part of anybody, an
intelligent and small job but a deeply exciting one.

Brown-Haired Secretary   I don't know why you want
me.

Head of Administration   We like you.

Brown-Haired Secretary   How do you know?

Female Managing Director   We just know.

Brown-Haired Secretary   Who talked to you about me?

Head of Administration   Everybody's talking about you, since the first day you entered the Company. We all envy your boss. Even the Chief Managing Director envies your boss.

Female Managing Director   Everybody envies you.

Brown-Haired Secretary   Everybody?

Female Managing Director   All your colleagues. Everybody wants you. You're the model employee, the fashionable employee.

Brown-Haired Secretary   I'm not worth a peseta. My head is a jumbled-up mixture of things and I'm strange.

Pause.

I'm useless.

Pause.

All I'm good for is thinking and dreaming, thinking up nonsense.

Female Managing Director   Fantastic! That's what we need!

Head of Administration   Somebody struggling to be a nobody.

Brown-Haired Secretary   I don't understand. I'm not struggling to be a nobody. I . . . I am a nobody.

Female Managing Director   You're extraordinary.

Brown-Haired Secretary   I suppose you don't want to leave until you've dealt with all the formalities of the company you want to set up.

Female Managing Director   Exactly.

Brown-Haired Secretary   That means months.

Female Managing Director   Everything's planned, eighteen months.

Brown-Haired Secretary   Look, a bird.

Pause.

All this must remain secret, of course.

Female Managing Director   Only the three of us know about it.

Brown-Haired Secretary   I might . . .

Female Managing Director   You won't do it.

Brown-Haired Secretary   No, of course not. I won't do it. I won't say anything. But I can't agree to be a part of your disgusting project.

Pause.

Female Managing Director   Disgusting?

Head of Administration   Do you feel comfortable in the Company?

Brown-Haired Secretary   No.

Head of Administration   So?

Female Managing Director   Listen, listen, we want something new, autonomous, small, free, self-managed, creative; basically, it's an ambitious project, we don't like the way they do business here, everything's pompous, impersonal, grey, ordinary. We want adventure, risk, excitement, passion, don't you understand?

Brown-Haired Secretary   No. What you want is . . .

Pause.

Head of Administration   What?

Brown-Haired Secretary   I don't know how to put it.

Female Managing Director   What's wrong with you?

Brown-Haired Secretary   Look, another bird.

Pause.

The first one was a male and this one's a female. They're different races. Do birds have races? Yes. They do. So, those two birds, of different races, have built a nest for themselves.

Look. They're flying. They hurtle down, in a free fall, and just a few inches from the ground they soar up, defying the laws of gravity. That's why they're birds. If I threw myself over the edge, I wouldn't be able to do that. I wouldn't be able to change my flight path a few inches from the ground to avoid crashing. I wouldn't be able to do it. I can't do anything against the laws of gravity. So, I know I'm not a bird.

Pause.

You aren't either, although you belong to a very different race from mine.

Exit the **Brown-Haired Secretary**.

Head of Administration   She's crazy.

Female Managing Director   She's delightful.

Pause.

I've got to have a smoke, I've got to have a smoke, smoke, smoke.

Head of Administration   What? You *do* smoke?

Female Managing Director   Yes, yes, yes, I smoke, what's wrong, eh?, don't you smoke?, well, I do too, yes, I do too, what's wrong, have you got anything against it?

Head of Administration   No, no, nothing, there's no need to shout.

The **Head of Administration** *gives her a cigarette and lights it.*

Female Managing Director   I want her.

Head of Administration   What?

Female Managing Director   I want her.

Head of Administration   Are you sure?

Female Managing Director   Aren't you?

Head of Administration   I don't know. Yes.

Female Managing Director   I can fly.

Head of Administration   What?

Female Managing Director   I can fly.

Head of Administration   I'm going.

Exit the **Head of Administration**. *The* **Female Managing Director** *goes up to the railing.*

Female Managing Director   I can fly I can fly I can fly I can fly I can fly . . .

The **Female Managing Director** *puts the cigarette in her mouth, hangs half of her body over the railing, opens her arms and closes her eyes.*

Scene 8

Enter the **Computer Programmer** *and the* **Local Messenger**.

Local Messenger   Today I can stay here all afternoon. There's no work to do. There's no work for me. Nobody sends parcels any more. Everybody sends letters. And fax machines never break down. If some day the postal service is improved they'll fire me, and if they fire me, I won't know what to do. I can't do anything else, I can't do anything. Carrying documents and parcels from one place to another in this city as quickly as possible. I like my job, but it has no future. On the other hand, you . . . Why don't you give me some lessons in computing?

Computer Programmer   I don't have enough time.

The **Local Messenger** *offers a cigarette to the* **Computer Programmer**. *They smoke.*

Local Messenger   Shame.

Pause.

Computer Programmer   Can I ask you a question?

Local Messenger   Yes.

Computer Programmer   What do you think of me?

Local Messenger   What?

Computer Programmer   What do you think of me?

Local Messenger   Well . . . I don't know, you're a pleasant, normal guy.

Computer Programmer   I mean physically.

Local Messenger   Well . . . Why do you ask?

Computer Programmer   I don't know.

Pause.

Because I'm worried.

Local Messenger   I see.

Computer Programmer   Obsessed.

Local Messenger   What with?

Computer Programmer   My physical appearance.

Local Messenger   I see. The thing is I'm hopeless about that sort of thing.

Computer Programmer   That's a shame.

Local Messenger   If you want to, I'll go and fetch my brother.

Computer Programmer   Your brother?

Local Messenger   Well, he's an expert in things to do with physical appearance.

Computer Programmer   I don't know him.

Local Messenger   Yes you do, he's the physiognomist who works during the evening shift.

Computer Programmer   Really? You're completely different.

Local Messenger   We're sons of the same mother.

Computer Programmer   I see.

Local Messenger   Do you want me to fetch him?

Computer Programmer   No, no, don't bother.

Pause.

So you don't know whether I look handsome or not?

Local Messenger   But why are you worried about that?

Computer Programmer   Because lately there's not a woman who isn't chasing me, especially the secretaries of the Company, they're all after me, they're constantly calling me, sometimes to ask me stupid questions they've just made up and they even damage a programme on purpose or erase the memory or block the keyboard, then I arrive and they stick to me, they talk to me in a low voice, they undress me with their eyes, they intimidate me, and that makes me sick, I feel ridiculous, and I feel like running, like running away, because I don't understand anything . . . because I don't consider myself attractive at all.

Local Messenger   Now that you say it, to tell you the truth, I think your incredibly ugly.

Computer Programmer   See? I told you.

Local Messenger   I mean it, really. I don't know if my opinion will help you.

Computer Programmer   Yes, it'll corroborate my theory.

Local Messenger   Which theory?

Computer Programmer   The uglier you feel, the more other people like you.

Local Messenger   A very original theory.

Computer Programmer   I like my job as well, but if I keep being at the mercy of the erotic impulses of twenty or thirty secretaries lusting for sex, I'll have to take measures.

Local Messenger   Listen, but why don't you take advantage of it?

Computer Programmer   I can't, I'm married.

Local Messenger   So what?

Computer Programmer   Don't you understand? I told you I'm married. I've got a wife, I've got my woman, I'm normal, I'm monogamous, OK? My wife is my wife and she's the only one, do you understand? There's no place for anything else in my head, only her, she makes the others vanish, do you understand?, she turns them into dust, into nothing, into negations of women, because she's not just another woman, because I always feel ugly but, funnily enough, I feel attractive when I'm with her, I know it's difficult to understand.

Local Messenger   Yes, a little. If I were in your place . . . phew! I would screw them all. Especially the red-haired one. Shit! She drives me fucking nuts.

Computer Programmer   She's ill.

Local Messenger   Yes, she's a bit of a pain when she explains her ideas and thinks she knows more than anybody else about everything, about the world, about life, when she talks about the hereafter and the hereinto, but I don't take any notice and don't listen to her, because I only look at her, and if I were in your place I'd wish that her computer broke down every two minutes, so I could repair it and, in passing, I'd do her a favour, I'd screw her for all I'm worth.

Computer Programmer   You're very young.

Local Messenger   Yes, but so are you.

Computer Programmer   Do you think I'm young?

Local Messenger   Of course! Listen, listen, can't you give me some lessons in computing? In return, I offer a Crash Course on Sexual Authority over Secretaries . . . Ha ha ha, I was obviously only joking.

Computer Programmer   I don't find it funny at all.

Local Messenger   Sorry.

Pause. He takes out his Digital Compact Cassette Player and puts on the headphones.

Americaaaaa!!

He takes out another pair of headphones, plugs them into the stereo and offers them to the **Computer Programmer**, *who puts them on. The* **Computer Programmer** *takes out a few folded sheets of paper. He tears them into pieces and drops them.*

Local Messenger   What's this?

Computer Programmer   Americaaaaa!!

Local Messenger   What are you doing?

Computer Programmer   What?!!

Local Messenger   What are these bits of paper?

Computer Programmer   Love letters from the secretaries.

Local Messenger   Give me some, I'll help you. And don't worry, right?, because I think you're appallingly ugly!

The **Computer Programmer** *gives some sheets to him. They both sing at the very tops of their voices as they tear the letters up. The pieces of paper, instead of falling, fly up in the air.*

Computer Programmer   They won't fall! They won't fall! They won't fall!

The **Local Messenger** *roars with laughter. The* **Computer Programmer** *bends his body over the edge to make the bits of paper fall. The* **Local Messenger** *gets frightened.*

Local Messenger   Hey!!!

Computer Programmer   What?

Local Messenger   Don't jump!!

Computer Programmer   What are you talking about? What a thing to say! I'm desperate, but not that desperate!

Local Messenger   Oh. Phew.

The **Computer Programmer** *laughs. They slap their hands, the American way. The noise of sirens is heard.*

Scene 9

Enter the **Dark-Haired Secretary**, *crying. She leans on the railing, takes out a cigarette and smokes. Enter the* **Brown-Haired Secretary**.

Dark-Haired Secretary   I've been changed to another department.

Brown-Haired Secretary   I know.

Dark-Haired Secretary   My boss has been dismissed.

Brown-Haired Secretary   I know.

Dark-Haired Secretary   Bribery, corruption, sexual harassment, they said.

Brown-Haired Secretary   It was true.

Dark-Haired Secretary   Yes, but he's a good man.

Brown-Haired Secretary   He was sick, he was an obsessed man.

Dark-Haired Secretary   I appreciate him. Why did you say he 'was'?

Brown-Haired Secretary   Don't pay any attention to me.

Dark-Haired Secretary   Do you want a fag?

Brown-Haired Secretary   Yes.

Dark-Haired Secretary   Here.

Brown-Haired Secretary   Thank you.

Dark-Haired Secretary   You're so strange. Sometimes you make me . . .

Brown-Haired Secretary   I think somebody's coming.

Pause.

No. Nobody's coming. I heard a noise.

Dark-Haired Secretary   I didn't.

Noise of broken glass. The **Brown-Haired Secretary** *looks down, over the railing.*

Brown-Haired Secretary   Look. Somebody's broken a window. Look.

Dark-Haired Secretary   It's my office!

Brown-Haired Secretary   It's him. Your boss. Look at him. He's gone out.

Dark-Haired Secretary   What does he want?

Brown-Haired Secretary   He's looking down.

Dark-Haired Secretary   What's he doing? Can't anybody stop him?

Brown-Haired Secretary   He's thinking about it.

We hear a long, loud scream, followed by the sound of something hitting the ground. Echo.

He's fallen.

Dark-Haired Secretary   He jumped!

Brown-Haired Secretary   He was an obsessed man, he was an obsessed man, he was sick.

Dark-Haired Secretary   I appreciated him.

Brown-Haired Secretary   I've got a headache.

Pause.

Poor man. How much was the fag?

Dark-Haired Secretary   Oh, nothing, it's a present.

The **Dark-Haired Secretary** *is about to leave. The* **Head of Administration** *runs on, panting. He looks at the* **Dark-Haired Secretary**.

Head of Administration   Did . . . did you see? . . . a colleague of mine . . . oh, your . . . your boss . . . did you see it? . . . I couldn't . . . I couldn't . . . do anything . . .

Dark-Haired Secretary   Did you try to stop him?

Head of Administration   Yes . . . yes, I couldn't do anything . . . I couldn't do anything.

Dark-Haired Secretary   Thank you.

The **Head of Administration** *and the* **Dark-Haired Secretary** *look at each other.*

Silence.

Head of Administration   Could you . . . could you, please . . . give me, I need it . . . a fag? . . .

The **Dark-Haired Secretary** *gives him a cigarette and light. They look at each other.*

Dark-Haired Secretary   Thank you.

The **Dark-Haired Secretary** *starts crying. The* **Head of Administration** *takes her in his arms.*

Brown-Haired Secretary   It should rain.

Scene 10

The **Red-Haired Secretary** *is smoking and looking over the edge. The* **Blonde Secretary** *creeps on and stands behind the* **Red-Haired Secretary**.

Blonde Secretary   Boo!

Red-Haired Secretary   Ah!, you scared me.

Blonde Secretary   I did it on purpose.

Red-Haired Secretary   You stupid woman.

Blonde Secretary   Look who's talking.

Red-Haired Secretary   Don't you realize I could have fallen?

Blonde Secretary   Come on, it was just a friendly joke, love.

Red-Haired Secretary   A friendly joke?

Blonde Secretary   Do you like looking down?

Red-Haired Secretary   Yes, it makes me think.

Blonde Secretary   It doesn't do anything for me, it
doesn't scare me, I don't like it particularly, it doesn't make
me think either. Look. A few days ago I was here, like this,
and I was thinking: if I fell, I'd die. They'd say: she fell, poor
girl. Or maybe: she jumped, like that subnormal idiot, the
Head of Personnel Recruitment, who got squashed, poor
thing. Oh no, no way, throwing myself over the edge doesn't
go with my character, does it?

Red-Haired Secretary   Someone throwing you over the
edge goes better with your character.

Blonde Secretary   You have such a special sense of
humour.

Red-Haired Secretary   I don't have any sense of
humour, love.

Blonde Secretary   Well, let's imagine that you're not
here, now, that I'm alone, here, and by chance, by a totally
fatal, totally stupid, totally whatever chance, I come up here
to look at the planes fly by, for instance, and I slip like the
idiot did the other day, but not on purpose like she did
(because she did it, you said so yourself, to attract people's
attention, the mediocrity), but just like this, because the
ground is slippery, for instance. What would happen? I'd fall
down, of course. And there we are!, everybody would say
that I jumped on purpose, they'd look for one thousand
excuses to justify my whatever it was: maybe she was one of
the mistresses of the Head of Personnel Recruitment, maybe
she was in love with her boss, maybe she was disgustingly
envious of the other secretaries, and especially of the
secretary of the Head of Public Relations, maybe she was
addicted and was found smoking on the roof, maybe she
wanted to shag the Computer Programmer, maybe she'd
slept with all the messengers in the Company, maybe she
flirted with all the executives to get a higher position, and so
on and so on . . . People are really evil-minded and bad!
Well, no, if I fell over it would be a coincidence, an accident,

I'd never jump, you get completely smashed when you crash against the ground, guess what my boss told me?

Red-Haired Secretary   What?

Blonde Secretary   He said that bodies explode inside. Do you believe it? I don't. Parachutists don't explode. On the rollercoasters nobody explodes. High divers don't explode. I can't see any link between a fall and an explosion, my idiot boss wants to impress me with disgusting stupidities and anything impresses me, but I've got a brain as well and I think too, his head did explode, poor man, since his wife dumped him for another man, poor thing, he doesn't know how to cover up the mess and he does it by trying to be unpleasant and rude to impress me, poor man. Listen, love, are you listening to me?

Red-Haired Secretary   No. I've got some problems. That's why I was thinking.

Blonde Secretary   Can I help you?

Red-Haired Secretary   I don't think so.

Blonde Secretary   What kind of problems? With your boss?

Red-Haired Secretary   No. Personal ones.

Blonde Secretary   Love problems, you mean.

Red-Haired Secretary   No. I don't know. I think I'm going through a crisis.

Blonde Secretary   I understand.

Red-Haired Secretary   Why did you want to throw yourself over the edge?

Blonde Secretary   Me? Did I say I wanted to throw myself?

Red-Haired Secretary   Yes, you've been talking all the time about throwing yourself over the edge.

Blonde Secretary   Goodness, love, how frightening you are. What kind of crisis are you going through?

150   After the Rain

Red-Haired Secretary   A crisis of values.

Blonde Secretary   Oh, oh, I think this is serious.

Red-Haired Secretary   I'm suffering.

Blonde Secretary   What's wrong with you?

Red-Haired Secretary   I hear voices, here, inside my head, voices of men, women, children, voices that are not mine and my head explodes. Mine really does explode. These voices tell me what I have to do, they dictate my words, my acts, do this, do that, say this, say that, they provoke me, these voices that I hear come from the outside and then I think it's not my head, that I'm a chosen one, a new Joan, chosen to tell the truth, so everybody will finally know the truth, a cataclysm is coming, a punishment, this drought, these two years of drought are a punishment from the cosmos, universal punishment, drought of the earth and drought of mankind, we are the earth, this is what these voices tell me, but although they come from the outside, I hear them here in my head and then I suffer I suffer I suffer because suddenly I think that everything is false and that these voices are mine and it's me who's saying all that to myself and nothing exists outside me so that means I'm crazy.

Blonde Secretary   Oh, oh, oh, don't you think that this thing you're going through is a bit simpler than that? I think what you need is a good screw, love, the only drought which is not good is the one down here, love, I know what I'm talking about. What's happening to you is very simple: the men you like think you're disgusting (I realized this a few days ago, with the Programmer, you can't deny you like him, and he thinks you're disgusting, doesn't he?), on the other hand, you don't like the men who like you and you ignore them and you think they're disgusting, for instance that boy, the messenger, that one who's so cute, he's crazy about you, he told me so yesterday, by the way, he fucks really well, I recommend him, I know he looks pathetic but he's a wild beast in bed, love, a wild beast, I bet you that in a single night this bloke can make all these stupidities in your head disappear.

Red-Haired Secretary   What's it like?

Blonde Secretary   Enormous.

Red-Haired Secretary   You never told me.

Blonde Secretary   You never asked me.

Red-Haired Secretary   Come on, these things aren't asked, friends tell each other without asking.

Blonde Secretary   Oh, so you and me are friends?

Red-Haired Secretary   We are, aren't we?

Blonde Secretary   Well, all right. Give me a kiss.

They kiss.

Now that we're friends, can I ask you a question?

Red-Haired Secretary   Yes.

Blonde Secretary   Are you a believer?

Red-Haired Secretary   No.

Blonde Secretary   The thing is you've got a reputation.

Red-Haired Secretary   It must be all the gossip, you've said so yourself lots of times, people are bad and evil-minded. I'm not a believer. I just have my theories, and my voices, of course. So it's enormous?

Blonde Secretary   Yes.

Red-Haired Secretary   So what should I do?

Blonde Secretary   Do you want to cure your illness? Shut up, somebody's coming.

Enter the **Local Messenger**.

Local Messenger   Oh. Hello. Sorry. I'll go.

Blonde Secretary   No, no, stay.

Red-Haired Secretary   Pull down your trousers and your pants.

The **Local Messenger** *drops his trousers and pants.*

Blonde Secretary   See? I told you.

Pause.

Red-Haired Secretary   Where are you going to invite me for dinner?

The **Local Messenger** *jumps for joy.*

Sound of a helicopter approaching. Wind. The **Local Messenger** *looks up, frightened.*

Local Messenger   Oh!

Red-Haired Secretary   Calm down, this one won't explode.

The helicopter moves away. The three of them remain still, the **Local Messenger** *with his trousers down.*

Suddenly, silence.

Scene 11

Enter the **Dark-Haired Secretary** *and the* **Brown-Haired Secretary***. They walk towards the railing. They look at each other. The* **Brown-Haired Secretary** *embraces the* **Dark-Haired Secretary***. They separate. They look at each other. The* **Dark-Haired Secretary** *nods. The* **Brown-Haired Secretary** *throws herself over the edge. A scream. Echo. The* **Dark-Haired Secretary** *coldly watches her fall.*

Dark-Haired Secretary   One, two, three. She's dead now. There's nobody in the street. Her sterile body is beginning to rot.

She lights a cigarette.

Transition.

The **Dark-Haired Secretary** *is smoking and looking over the edge. Enter the* **Brown-Haired Secretary***.*

Brown-Haired Secretary   Hello.

Dark-Haired Secretary   Ah!

Brown-Haired Secretary   Did I scare you?

Dark-Haired Secretary   Oh. Yes. Oh.

Brown-Haired Secretary   What's wrong.

Dark-Haired Secretary   I was dreaming! I was
dreaming!

Brown-Haired Secretary   I'm sorry.

Dark-Haired Secretary   No, no, I should be sorry.

Brown-Haired Secretary   I came for a breath of fresh
air.

Dark-Haired Secretary   Are you nervous?

Brown-Haired Secretary   No.

Dark-Haired Secretary   I was thinking about you. I've
just been told the news. If I was in your place I'd be nervous.
That's amazing. It's the first time a thing like this has
happened since . . .

Brown-Haired Secretary   Since when?

Dark-Haired Secretary   I don't know. I've been
working here for more than six months and I'd never seen
anything like this, this is unprecedented, I'd never have said
a thing like this could happen in a company like this, really,
congratulations, congratulations, I don't know what to say,
really, everybody's talking about it, it's the main news of the
day, the main news of the month, you're the main news of the
year, I don't know what you expect me to say, I was even
dreaming about you!

Brown-Haired Secretary   Don't say anything.

Dark-Haired Secretary   I think everybody's in a state.
And not exactly a good one, especially our colleagues.

Brown-Haired Secretary   I know.

Dark-Haired Secretary   So now what will you do?

Brown-Haired Secretary   I don't know.

Dark-Haired Secretary   I still find it hard to believe. Well now, everybody knew that you . . . I mean, all the people in our department knew perfectly that you . . .

Brown-Haired Secretary   That I?

Dark-Haired Secretary   That you were different, you are different.

Brown-Haired Secretary   What does that mean?

Dark-Haired Secretary   Don't make me say it, you know so better than anybody else. You're different, you are . . . you are . . . I think that those at the top knew it from the first moment. A jump like this can't be improvised in one day. The Chief Managing Director must have had something to do with it, he's a very good friend of your boss, the Head of Public Relations, sorry, I should say your *ex*-boss.

Brown-Haired Secretary   A jump?

Dark-Haired Secretary   Don't you think this is a jump?

Brown-Haired Secretary   I don't think it's anything.

Dark-Haired Secretary   Sorry, I don't know whether I should keep on talking to you so casually.

Brown-Haired Secretary   Of course you should.

Dark-Haired Secretary   But everything will change now.

Brown-Haired Secretary   I don't know.

Dark-Haired Secretary   Now you have power.

Brown-Haired Secretary   I had it before, as well. Without any position. Power is not about posts, it's not a question of positions or values, or scales, or scales of values. Real power is in eyes and words, power is in gesture and in silence, it is not in an office, or on a piece of paper, or a dress or money, it is not in anything you can measure. Power is not measurable. And eyes cannot lie, they don't know how to hide; misleading words end up betraying whoever pronounces them; temperamental, uncontrolled, hysterical gestures, twitches, contraction of the muscles, tension of bodies, false movements, discomfort in your own body and the discomfort of the silence after an argument: these are the miseries of the ones with fake power. Honest eyes, free speech, still gestures, patient silence: that's my power, and I've had it for a long time.

Dark-Haired Secretary   You scare me.

Brown-Haired Secretary   That's not true. You like me.

Dark-Haired Secretary   That's not true.

Brown-Haired Secretary   Yes it is.

Dark-Haired Secretary   I'm weak.

Brown-Haired Secretary   So am I.

Dark-Haired Secretary   I'm weak and I envy you, if only you knew what I was dreaming about.

Brown-Haired Secretary   Some day you'll have children and I'll envy you.

Dark-Haired Secretary   What?

Brown-Haired Secretary   I've had it.

Dark-Haired Secretary   What?

Brown-Haired Secretary   I can't have children, I'm sterile.

Dark-Haired Secretary   Oh.

Enter the **Female Managing Director**.

Female Managing Director   I knew you were here!

Dark-Haired Secretary   Are you talking to me?

Female Managing Director   What did you do, you fucking hole, what did you do, you rotten bitch, you shit-sucking climber, I'd like to know whose arse you licked, whose arse did you have to lick, you bitch, bitch, fucking bitch, what I've just been told about you can't be true, a vulgar, lunatic Public Relations secretary, you lunatic, stupid, hypocritical, hollow, fucking ambitious traitor, is it

true that in this shitty company, in this shitty city, in this
shitty country, in this shitty world a low-class secretary can
become, overnight, Assistant to the Chief Managing
Director in one of the most profitable financial companies in
this city, in this country, in this continent, in the world, in the
universe? Is what I've just been told true? Tell me it isn't,
now that you're here, come on, tell me it isn't, tell me it's not
true with your own mouth, with your own smelly mouth,
because if it is true, I'll throw myself over the edge right now
to protest against it . . . what? and she still has the nerve to
laugh, fucking bitch!, she still has the nerve to laugh at me
the same way she laughed at everybody, let's see now, how
many dicks, how many arses, how many cunts did you have
to clean with your poisonous tongue, with your bitch slobber
to make this possible, let's see, how many?!!!

Dark-Haired Secretary   Excuse me . . . don't you think
that . . . ?

Female Managing Director   And you shut up, you idiot,
you're worse than her, we all know you defend her, that
you're in love with her, shut up, you idiot, shut up, give me a
fag and go away.

Brown-Haired Secretary (*to the* **Dark-Haired
Secretary**)   Stay. (*To the* **Female Managing Director**.)
Hello, good afternoon. I don't think we've met. At least, not
officially. From now on we'll have to work together. I guess
the Chief Managing Director will call a special Board
Meeting tomorrow to award me my new position. I think
you're one of the members of the Board, if I'm not mistaken.
Obviously, you'll be able to make any complaints
concerning my appointment tomorrow. I can introduce the
matter myself so it doesn't cause you any inconvenience. Do
you agree? All right. It's been a pleasure. Oh, forgive me if I
offended you by my laughter. Sometimes it just comes out, I
can't help it. Mind you, usually I'm not cheerful at all, just
the opposite. The thing is I've always found people who
describe themselves by insulting others very funny. Have a
nice day.

Exit the **Female Managing Director**.

Dark-Haired Secretary   She's gone crazy.

Brown-Haired Secretary   That's right, I'm sterile. The doctors confirmed it yesterday. It seems impossible, doesn't it? It seems impossible nowadays. I've tried everything. Everything. Believe me, I've tried everything. They thought I had a malformation in my womb. But they were wrong. The last doctor I visited told me yesterday that my ovaries secrete a strange substance that prevents fertilization. I can't explain it. He was talking about antibodies. They act as a kind of spermicide. He says the only hope is finding the sperm of a man who's immune to this substance, to these antibodies. There's a probability of one in a million. I won't find him. You see, I've got everything and I don't have what I most want: the child of one man in a million. You see, I'm not happy. I'm scared. I'm alone. Soon, my sterile body will begin to rot.

Dark-Haired Secretary   Don't say that, don't say that!

Brown-Haired Secretary   And I'll be alone. I wish I was dead.

Dark-Haired Secretary   Shut up.

Brown-Haired Secretary   Are you crying?

Dark-Haired Secretary   Do you believe in dreams?

Brown-Haired Secretary   No.

Dark-Haired Secretary   You must believe in them. Believe in dreams. You'll find that man.

Enter the **Female Managing Director**.

Female Managing Director   People who describe themselves by insulting others?!!!!

She goes towards the **Brown-Haired Secretary** *with the intention of clawing at her, but the* **Dark-Haired Secretary** *blocks her way.*

Dark-Haired Secretary   Don't you touch her, do you hear me?

Female Managing Director   Get away.

Dark-Haired Secretary   You won't touch her while I'm here.

Female Managing Director   Just watch me!

She tries to go towards the **Brown-Haired Secretary**. *The* **Dark-Haired Secretary** *stops her. They fight. They fall on the ground. They pull each other's hair and claw at each other. The* **Brown-Haired Secretary** *goes towards the railing and looks over the edge.*

Brown-Haired Secretary   Everything seems so small from here. So ridiculous.

She dribbles a stream of saliva over the edge.

Scene 12

Enter the **Blonde Secretary** *and the* **Red-Haired Secretary**. *They each light a cigarette.*

Blonde Secretary   Maybe this one will be the last one.

Red-Haired Secretary   Do you think so?

Blonde Secretary   I don't know exactly what's happening, but I know something serious is happening, what do you think? what's your theory?

Red-Haired Secretary   Theory? I don't understand you.

Blonde Secretary   But, love, what's wrong with you?, you don't seem the same.

Red-Haired Secretary   Really?

Blonde Secretary   Oh, everybody's ill, everybody's in a terrible state. Do you know why I told you this one will be the last one?

Red-Haired Secretary   No.

Blonde Secretary   The Head of Personnel made me go to
his office and told me that he wanted to punish me by
suspending my salary for three months for having come up
here to smoke, he says that he knows exactly who we are and
that he's watching us; I immediately realized what was going
on, I realized what had happened, because I'm really shrewd
about these things, you know, and I told him, completely
naturally: oh, I didn't know you were a poofter as well!; the
bloke opened his eyes like this and shut up, I took advantage
of him not speaking and said: so you scored with that big
mouth, the lift-attendant? that's bad kid, very bad, I told
him, because that baby's pulling your leg, can't you realize
it?, don't you see he's known for a long time that a few of us
come up here to smoke and he's waited to score with you to
give the tip-off at the right moment?, that baby is a climber,
I'm telling you, and he's using you to get the position of Head
of Personnel Recruitment, let me see, let me see, I said, I'm
sure you have some piece of paper around here on the table
with his application!, and I started grabbing all the papers
on his table. Oh, you should have seen his face! What a mess.
He started to choke and stammer three or four words, he said
no, no, I won't punish you but get out of my office. But that's
nothing, love, that's nothing, I haven't told you the most
interesting news, yet. I just went out of his office and met my
boss crying, my boss crying!, him, the one who's always
saying that crying is unaesthetic, and so on, imagine him
with his eyes full of sleep, they were red, really red, his nose
full of green snot and his mouth with little bubbles of saliva
and a trickle of spittle falling down onto the lapel of his
jacket, another mess; I asked him what's the matter, boss?
and he told me that he had just been denied legal paternity of
his daughter and that he wanted to turn into a vegetable, I
want to be a carrot! I want to be a carrot!, he said, imagine it,
poor man, I knew he would end up going crazy, him too; but
wait, love, that's not all, I walked my boss to the toilets to
relieve his diarrhoea and I met the Personnel Recruitment
secretary, the dark-haired one, the vulgar one, her face
covered in blood, my darling!, I said, you look as though
you've been fighting a lion, a lioness!, she answered, a

fucking bitch who scratched her nails down my face!, and it
turned out that the lioness fucking bitch was none other than
your boss, and when I asked her why she had done that to
her, she said because of having defended the Public Relations
secretary who, and now listen carefully, love, listen carefully
because this is a bombshell: she's promoted to Assistant
Director of the Company!, yes, love, yes, I nearly had a
breakdown as well, they've gone crazy, installing a
philosopher as the Assistant Big Boss!, a nutter!, where are we
going to end up, I thought, I didn't say a word, of course, not
a word to the dark-haired one, who, I bet my life on it, will be
appointed Head of Personnel Recruitment tomorrow,
directly, because everybody knows that those two defend
each other and go around everywhere together, now you're
definitely done for, I thought, oh, poor me and my friend, I
thought (I said friend referring to you, love, to you),
considering how she dislikes us, that philosopher, oh dear,
she'll fire us, and so on, and so on, I didn't say all this to
anybody, no, no, of course not, that would be the limit, I was
just thinking about it, and I thought, damn!, we're in a really
bad situation! and, as I was going towards my office to
recover from the shock, I met the Programmer, the good-
looking one, the stupid one, with his face distorted, all dirty,
his hair messed up, his eyes looking wild, oh my God!,
another one who's gone crazy, then, to brighten up the
situation, to have some fun, which in these situations is
always good and calms everything down, I said, where are
you going with that face, man?, you look as if you'd just been
to a funeral, and he gave me such a terrible, such a big slap on
my face that I bit my tongue and look, love, look what a
blister I got, and then he ran away screaming hysterically,
shouting a woman's name that I'd never heard before; two
minutes later, while I was recovering from that smack,
someone told me that what is wrong with him is that he's
desperate because his wife had died yesterday, murdered,
tortured and raped by seven lads while she was going for a
quiet walk in the street at six o'clock in the evening, of course,
then I understood his reaction, but love, I didn't know
anything, I swear, and I quickly started looking for him to

apologize for having said that thing about the funeral, and I found him lying down in the middle of the corridor, unconscious, and nobody helped him. Then, I remembered what you told me a few days ago and that's why I came to see you, to tell you, love, I need to talk to you, to let off steam, and that's what I wanted to tell you, love: I think what you told me is true and I'm scared.

Red-Haired Secretary   What did I say.

Blonde Secretary   You said a cataclysm is coming.

Red-Haired Secretary   Did I say that?

Blonde Secretary   Yes.

Red-Haired Secretary   Oh.

Blonde Secretary   What do you think?

Red-Haired Secretary   I was talking about the sky.

Blonde Secretary   The sky?

Red-Haired Secretary   I meant a flood is coming.

Blonde Secretary   A what?

Red-Haired Secretary   Nothing, nothing, forget it.

Blonde Secretary   Listen, love, you're very relaxed, aren't you?

Red-Haired Secretary   Really?

Blonde Secretary   Really.

Red-Haired Secretary   It's just that I don't hear voices any more.

Blonde Secretary   Oh.

Suddenly, the **Computer Programmer** *enters, moving almost like a sleepwalker.*

Computer Programmer   Has anybody seen my wife around here?

Blonde Secretary   Ah! Ah, you scared me. Oh, by the way, now that you're here, I'd like to apologize for . . .

The **Red-Haired Secretary** *takes the* **Blonde Secretary** *by the arm and forces her to shut up. The* **Computer Programmer** *walks towards the railing with his eyes fixed in a stare. When he is really close to the railing, the voice of the* **Red-Haired Secretary** *stops him.*

Red-Haired Secretary   Don't do it!

Pause.

I advise you not to do it. Look, over there. The sky. I know you don't believe me. You think I'm crazy. But just for once, believe me. Look at the sky. In a short time it'll start raining.

Computer Programmer   Yes, it should rain.

Pause.

Lightning.

Scene 13

Enter the **Head of Administration** *and the* **Female Managing Director**.

Head of Administration   Let's have a smoke.

Female Managing Director   No.

Head of Administration   Well, I'm going to, I'm going to because I feel like it.

The **Head of Administration** *takes out a cigarette and smokes.*

Female Managing Director   What are we going to do.

Head of Administration   Nothing.

Female Managing Director   She's a traitor, a slimy climber.

Head of Administration   I don't think so.

Female Managing Director   I hate you as well. You defend her as well.

Head of Administration   Yes. Me too. I'm more or less like everybody else.

Female Managing Director   But what about our company?

Head of Administration   What company?

Female Managing Director   We need . . .

Head of Administration   Nothing. Nothing at all. *You* need. Only *you* need. I don't need anything. Anything at all. I'm giving up.

Female Managing Director   What?!

Head of Administration   I give up, I'm staying here, I know everything will change, everything will change from now on, I know, I have confidence in that woman, and you know I don't have any ambition, I don't have false hopes any more, I'm staying here.

Female Managing Director   Do you know what you are? Do you want me to tell you? You're a coward. A ridiculous, little, insignificant coward. You're weak.

Head of Administration   And you're too strong. I'm fed up with strong women, I can't stand it, I can't stand it any more, I can't bear women who are too strong, you're just like her, like many others, you're all too strong, you're stronger than men, we men should give birth and you women should run the businesses, I've realized, I've realized exactly , so many years working and, see, now I realize I'm not fit to work, I'm not strong enough, you see?, my mother wasn't strong, she was one of the last women I knew, I mean, one of the last real women, one of the submissive women, at least on the surface, a woman without an official job, I mean, her only job was giving birth to me and to my brothers and putting the food in our mouths and cleaning our shit, she seemed happy, my mother, you know?, but she was weak, she was easy to deceive, she was inactive, we used to call her the carrot, because she always said that it was on the ground that she felt well, quiet, resting, and she died, and she died saying,

'I've been happy, my son,' and she was nothing, she was nobody, she didn't want anything either, anything but a simple carrot, she wasn't like you, like any of you, any of you, and now I want to be my mother, I want to close myself up, I want to be nothing, I want to be an old-fashioned woman, I'm alone, my ex-wife, I should say ex-husband, ex-wife-husband, has just stolen what was left of the man in me and I have nothing left, I'm nothing now, and when I look at you I see her and I loathe you, I hate you, I hate your projects, your small-huge company, I hate your power, your strength, your face, your hands, your man's perfume, I hate your voice and your eyes and I just want to smoke, smoke, smoke, smoke, smoke, to stay here and to look at the landscape!

Female Managing Director   You're a rat.

Head of Administration   Not even that. I'm a carrot.

Female Managing Director   A rat. A cornered rat. You don't even move me to pity.

Head of Administration   You're the rat. Cornered by yourself, by your pride, by your virility. A woman has defeated you, a real woman, with her intelligence, or maybe rather, her sensitivity. Now she's occupying the position she really deserves, above you, and you can't stand it. The man you are is rebelling and falling over the edge.

Female Managing Director   I'll be able to do it on my own. I don't need you. You or her. As far as I'm concerned, you can throw yourself down, to the ground below, since that's where you want to stay. Jump, come on, I'd do it if I were you, a machine can do your work perfectly, you're unnecessary, do you understand me?, you're in the way in this world, so jump, come on, jump, you cuckold!, you cuckold!, you cuckold!

The **Head of Administration** *slaps her in the face.*

Female Managing Director   I want to have a smoke, I've got to have a smoke!

The **Head of Administration** *slaps her in the face again.*

Female Managing Director   I don't like anything. I don't feel good with anybody. I do my things properly. I'm fit for work. I was brought up to work. You can't work properly, here. I just want to be happy. Working. With work that suits me, I mean it, I don't have any other ambitions. I want some dignity. I need dignity. That's why I want to be on top. I want to leave this place. I'm good. I'm a good person. A clever and intelligent person, but not very sensitive. I just need someone who's sensitive. Like you. Like that traitor. Help me. Help me to leave this place.

Head of Administration   No. I can't. I want to be alone.

Female Managing Director   That's not true.

A thunderclap.

Head of Administration   It wasn't an explosion.

Female Managing Director   Yes it was.

Head of Administration   No. I think it's a storm.

Exit **Female Managing Director**. *The* **Head of Administration** *stays, looking at the sky. Another thunderclap. The* **Head of Administration** *closes his eyes and smiles.*

Scene 14

Enter the **Local Messenger** *and the* **Computer Programmer**. *During the whole scene there is the noise of people rushing around, cars, sirens. The noise of intermittent planes, helicopters, lights. There is a strange excitement in the atmosphere. Looking at the sky, one can notice that, for the first time, it is about to rain.*

Local Messenger   Come with me, don't stay here. Come on, lean on me, we can't miss this, can we? Come on, cheer up, cheer up, we'll smoke a cigarette, OK?

Computer Programmer   Yes. A cigarette. Yes.

Local Messenger   There, take it. Mmm . . . This way, if
we have a smoke, it won't seem as though we're waiting so
long, will it? They didn't specify the exact time, but judging
by the way the sky looks . . . I don't think it will be long. I
arranged to meet here with my girlfriend, you know, the one
who's hot stuff . . . heh heh heh, but don't worry, I told her I
would make you come up here if I met you, because I say so,
man, because I like you, full stop, there's no other reason,
and also because I can't let you go home on a day like this, so
you start worrying and all that, and although you never got
on well with her, she said that it was OK, that, when it comes
down to it, she feels sor . . . she'll probably turn up.

Computer Programmer   Your girlfriend predicted it.

Local Messenger   Yes, the thing is she's very intuitive,
heh heh heh, she's a great girl.

Computer Programmer   You look as though you've
fallen in love with her.

Local Messenger   I do, don't I? I think I have. Well,
there's nothing I can do about it, is there? That's the way it
goes, first you see a bum and you like it and you want to touch
it, and you think: when I've touched it, right, let's find
another one, but no, it turns out that one fine day, even
though you don't exactly intend to, you touch that bum and
you say, damn, this bum isn't like the others, and then you
realize that bum belongs to a girl who's got a pair of eyes and
you go and look at her eyes and think, shit, I'd never paid any
attention to a girl's eyes, then you stop looking at her bum
and you only want to look at her eyes, and then you know
you're done for, and you don't want the girl to get away
because you love her eyes and you're afraid you'll never find
another pair of eyes like those and you're afraid this thing
that's happening to you won't happen ever again.

Computer Programmer   By the way, have you seen my
wife around here?

Local Messenger   What? Come on, shut up, OK?, shut
up and smoke and look at the sky and don't think about

anything else, OK?, it's about to happen and we can't miss it
. . . phew.

Enter the **Dark-Haired Secretary**.

Dark-Haired Secretary   The time has come.

Local Messenger   Oh, hello!

Dark-Haired Secretary   Has anybody seen the new
Managing Director?

Local Messenger   No. Not me.

Computer Programmer   And you? . . . Have you seen
my wife?

Silence. The **Dark-Haired Secretary** *and the* **Local
Messenger** *glance at each other. The* **Computer
Programmer** *notices and exits.*

Local Messenger   He's in a terrible state, I don't know
what to say to him.

Dark-Haired Secretary   I've noticed. Give me a fag.

The **Local Messenger** *gives her a cigarette. The* **Blonde
Secretary** *rushes on.*

Blonde Secretary   Oh, I'm so nervous. As I climbed the
stairs I kept asking myself whether I'm happy or sad it's
going to rain. I mean, it's been such a long time that I don't
remember whether I liked it or not, hee hee hee, oh, that's
funny. By the way, has anybody seen my boss?

Dark-Haired Secretary   No. Is he coming?

Blonde Secretary   Yes, he told me he didn't want to miss
it, and that he'd come up here, listen, you, you look very . . .
like that, you know?, very happy. Why are you so happy,
you're always sad?

Enter the **Red-Haired Secretary**. *She goes straight to the* **Local
Messenger**, *throws herself on him and kisses him on the mouth
passionately.*

Red-Haired Secretary   Let's get out of this place, let's go,
let's go, come on!

Local Messenger   What are you saying? Now you want to go?

Red-Haired Secretary   Yes.

Local Messenger   But where?

Red-Haired Secretary   Out of here, far from here.

She kisses him again.

Blonde Secretary   Hello, love, did you notice me?

Red-Haired Secretary   Hello.

Blonde Secretary   You look a bit euphoric as well.

Red-Haired Secretary   Yes, yes, I want to go, we've got to get out of this place.

Blonde Secretary   So where do you want to go, now?

Red-Haired Secretary   Now? Not now, forever.

Local Messenger   What are you saying?

Red-Haired Secretary   Let's go, please, let's go, my heart is telling me to, my heart, no, no, don't be afraid, I don't intend making up a theory, I don't have anything in my head, my head hasn't told me anything, now it's something different, it's an impulse coming from here, inside here, it's not words, it's not voices, nobody's dictating anything to me, it's something different, a kind of need, I know I've got to leave everything behind, I just quit my job, I'm happy, I feel well, I want to get out of this place, I feel like laughing, now that I feel well I realize that everybody here has gone crazy and I feel like laughing, my boss has resigned, she's furious with me because she wanted me to go with her, I told her I wouldn't and I feel well, I don't want to work, we don't have to work, let's go, I feel as if I'd been released from an enormous burden I was carrying without realizing it, let's go, I want the rain to catch us far from here, where there's nobody at all.

She kisses the **Local Messenger** *again.*

Blonde Secretary   I told you your problem was different, love.

Local Messenger (*to the* **Red-Haired Secretary**)   You'll always be a radical.

Enter the **Female Managing Director**. *She walks straight towards the* **Blonde Secretary**, *without looking at anybody else. The* **Local Messenger** *and the* **Red-Haired Secretary** *continue kissing each other passionately during the whole scene. The* **Dark-Haired Secretary** *looks at the sky with a smile on her face.*

Female Managing Director   Do you want to be my secretary? Or are you another stupid slimy company climber or a hypocritical traitor who's not content with such an exciting and decent job as yours and whose only aim is being something else than that without even having the minimum, basic abilities essential to do so?

Blonde Secretary   Well, right away . . .

Female Managing Director   The thing is I'm leaving the Company, you know? I've given up my position. Exactly one hour, five minutes ago. You've got three seconds to think about it. We'll start work tomorrow. You and me. The two of us alone. My idea is simple. Any small company, whatever it is, it doesn't really matter, with no overriding desire for profit-making, only with a competitive desire, for the pleasure of working, for the pleasure of knowing and feeling that we are real leaders in our job. I don't know which one yet but, if you feel like it, we can talk about it right now and choose the one we prefer, I don't really mind, choose it yourself: image advising, financial advising, legal advising, control and personnel recruitment, company promotion, industrial pre-production, post-production, management, advertising design, publicity control for companies, inservice and private education, computer programming, computer technical assistance, business administrative agency, estate agents, insurance company, loan service for first and second mortgage, property administration, invoicing, credits, psychotechnological, psychometrical or mnemotechnic services, psychological clinic, welfare work, artistic patronage, literary or matrimonial agency, school of aesthetics, relax-massage centre, contacts, which one do you prefer?

Blonde Secretary   Contacts. I want to be your secretary.

Female Managing Director   I'd like to have enough strength and courage to kill myself, but I don't.

Blonde Secretary   Don't talk nonsense. Now you've got me. We'll start straight away tomorrow. And we'll stick at it, don't worry. I've got very good friends. Male and female.

Female Managing Director   Really?

Blonde Secretary   Yes.

Female Managing Director   Tell me, now that we'll work together and we'll have to put up with each other, what do you think of me?

Blonde Secretary   You're good-looking, intelligent and a bit manly.

Female Managing Director   But you don't think I'm sensitive, do you?

Blonde Secretary   Well, yes, maybe just a little bit, yes, sensitive as well.

Female Managing Director   Thank you. So, what are we going to do?

Blonde Secretary   Let's leave, let's go downstairs, downstairs, people are going crazy here, and all the more so now, with the rain coming, and we've got a lot of work to do, haven't we?

Female Managing Director   Excuse me, did you say a moment ago that you think I'm good-looking?

Blonde Secretary   Did I say that?

Female Managing Director   I think you did.

Blonde Secretary   Are you married?

Female Managing Director   No.

Blonde Secretary   Me neither. Don't you have a partner?

Female Managing Director   No. I don't like partners, I like businesses. What about you?

Blonde Secretary   Well, I don't know, I like being a secretary best of all. Maybe we were made for each other, I don't know.

Female Managing Director   I think you're a calming influence.

Blonde Secretary   Shall we have a cigarette?

Female Managing Director   Yes. The last one.

Blonde Secretary   The last one? Don't you believe it!, woman, don't you believe it! The first one!

Female Managing Director   Oh.

Blonde Secretary   Aren't we leaving this company? So let's smoke, woman, let's smoke, we don't need to hide any more, and they can all get stuffed!

Female Managing Director   Yes, you definitely calm me down.

They light cigarettes and smoke them. The **Local Messenger** *and the* **Red-Haired Secretary** *are still kissing each other in the background. Enter the* **Brown-Haired Secretary**.

Dark-Haired Secretary   Hello. I was looking for you.

Brown-Haired Secretary   Me? I don't feel well. I don't know what I came here for. Can it be true?

Dark-Haired Secretary   Of course it can. Don't you want to stay?

Brown-Haired Secretary   I don't know. There's so much electricity . . .

Dark-Haired Secretary   Do you want a fag?

Brown-Haired Secretary   I don't feel well.

Exit the **Brown-Haired Secretary**. *She passes the* **Head of Administration**, *who enters stealthily.*

Head of Administration   Not yet?

Blonde Secretary   Oh, hello boss, by the way, I have to tell you something . . .

Female Managing Director   Forget it.

The **Head of Administration** *looks at the* **Female Managing Director** *and the* **Blonde Secretary** *and goes towards the* **Dark-Haired Secretary**.

Head of Administration   Have you seen the Computer Programmer?

Dark-Haired Secretary   Yes, he left a moment ago.

Head of Administration   I'm afraid he might do something silly. The business with his wife has affected him so much.

Dark-Haired Secretary   I know.

Head of Administration   He was so excited about her. Poor naïve man. I will never leave my wife, he told me. He wanted to have a child. Where did he go?

Dark-Haired Secretary   I don't know.

Head of Administration   Your friend, the new Managing Director, she looked a bit annoyed.

Dark-Haired Secretary   Annoyed? No, I don't think so. I don't know what's wrong with her, I'm worried about her too, maybe she works too much, although I don't think that's her problem, no, that's not her problem. She doesn't feel well. A moment ago she admitted she was a bit nervous about the rain coming, she's always said that these two and a half years of drought have been very bad for us, she also said that if it didn't rain today, she was afraid it would never rain again. I'm worried about her, she was saying strange things, but I understand her. You know? I know her secret and her desire, if you knew . . . I'm ashamed to admit it, but I love . . .

Lightning. Thunder. Everybody looks at the sky.

Red-Haired Secretary   Let's go.

Local Messenger   Let's go, yes. Goodbye everybody. But, listen, listen, where are we going?

Red-Haired Secretary   Do you want me to tell you? To the countryside!

Local Messenger   What?!

Red-Haired Secretary   Yes, yes, to the countryside!!

Local Messenger   Have you gone crazy?

Red-Haired Secretary   To the countryside, to the countryside, to the countryside!, my heart is telling me 'go to the countryside!, to nature!'.

Local Messenger   Listen, love, listen, do you know how to get there?

Enter the **Computer Programmer**. *He drifts around the place. Lightning. Thunder.*

Computer Programmer   The rain.

Blonde Secretary (*to the* **Head of Administration**)
Boss, look, listen, I'm going with her.

Female Managing Director   Goodbye, loser.

Enter the **Brown-Haired Secretary**. *Lighning. Thunder.*

Brown-Haired Secretary   Let it be true, let it be true, let it be true . . .

Local Messenger   Well, fine, why not? . . . to the countryside!

General mobilization. The **Local Messenger** *with the* **Red-Haired Secretary** *and the* **Female Managing Director**, *walking arm-in-arm with the* **Blonde Secretary**, *all leave.*

Suddenly, the **Brown-Haired Secretary** *and the* **Computer Programmer** *meet in the middle of the roof and stare at each other. Lightning. Thunder.*

Head of Administration (*to the* **Dark-Haired Secretary**)   Are you scared?

Dark-Haired Secretary   I don't know. Maybe. A bit.

Head of Administration   Do you want to come with me?

Dark-Haired Secretary   What about them?

Head of Administration   Them? I think they've just discovered each other. Don't you want to come with me?

Dark-Haired Secretary   Ask me again, please.

Head of Administration   Come with me.

Dark-Haired Secretary   But first I just want to tell you one thing.

Head of Administration   Go on.

Dark-Haired Secretary   I'm a normal person.

The **Head of Administration** *puts an arm round her shoulders and holds her tight. They look at the* **Computer Programmer** *and the* **Brown-Haired Secretary** *and leave.*

The **Computer Programmer** *and the* **Brown-Haired Secretary** *keep staring at each other.*

Silence.

Computer Programmer   I've lost my wife.

Brown-Haired Secretary   Are you a man in a million?

The rain falls, silently.

They stay motionless, looking at each other, in the rain.

Epilogue: After the Rain

A year has passed.

A year of continuous rain. It's the early evening. The first day that it has not rained for a year.

The skyscraper has not resisted the erosion of the rain. A view of the roof displays a distressing landscape, looking like the top of a partly melted candle. Wear and tear, rust, breakages, filth.

Enter the **Brown-Haired Secretary** *and the* **Computer Programmer**. *Despite the passing of time, they both look younger now. She is pregnant.*

Computer Programmer   Is it here?

Brown-Haired Secretary   Yes.

Computer Programmer   What a strange place.

Brown-Haired Secretary   Yes.

Computer Programmer   Years ago, when I was a child, buildings used to withstand the wind and the rain.

Brown-Haired Secretary   I can hardly remember.

Computer Programmer   Yes you can.

Brown-Haired Secretary   I don't know.

Pause.

Years ago, when we were children, it didn't rain for a whole year. Then it didn't stop raining for two years in a row. Or maybe it did. Maybe I don't want to remember.

Computer Programmer   It's cold.

Brown-Haired Secretary   Is it?

Computer Programmer   Yes.

Brown-Haired Secretary   It's not cold. Maybe it's the effect of this . . .

Pause.

Desolation.

Pause.

But I like it.

Computer Programmer   Well, what are we doing here, can you tell me now?

Brown-Haired Secretary   I thought everybody would come.

Computer Programmer   Everybody?

Brown-Haired Secretary   Yes, everybody, don't you remember?

Computer Programmer   No.

Brown-Haired Secretary   Yes. You remember. We stopped coming up here that afternoon, when the rain came, two weeks before the Company was moved. Of course you remember. When they announced yesterday that the rain would finally stop, I suddenly felt the need to remember that afternoon, those days, they were days of hysteria, yes, you do remember.

Computer Programmer   The only thing I remember is that I didn't know you and I met you. It was here, wasn't it? Yes, the first day of rain.

Brown-Haired Secretary   Now the rain has stopped and there's nobody. Nobody's come back.

The **Computer Programmer** *embraces the* **Brown-Haired Secretary** *and caresses her belly.*

Computer Programmer   We . . . three came back, because you wanted to, and I can assure you there's two of us who don't know why.

Brown-Haired Secretary   I wanted to see this before the building is demolished.

Computer Programmer   Demolished?

Brown-Haired Secretary   Yes, didn't you know?

Computer Programmer   No.

Brown-Haired Secretary   Yes. In a few months' time. It'll be dynamited. The day they do it I want to come and see it. You'll come as well, and our child as well. We'll watch it from a distance. Won't we? We can watch it . . . we can watch it, for example . . . from there!, come, see?, yes, yes, what do you think?, from that house. Can you see that house?, the one that's made of stone, the one with wooden windows, the one with just three floors, can you see it? . . . I remember one day, in one of the windows, there

was a married woman who was dreaming about an
unknown man. The unknown man appeared one day when
the husband wasn't there and they made love like animals.
It turned out that, in a few days' time, while the husband
was having buttered toast and white coffee for breakfast,
the unknown man came back to see the lady and, between
the two of them, they made the husband leave the house.
Now they live together, very far from here, and they don't
have white coffee and buttered toast for breakfast. They
just don't have breakfast, because when they wake up
they're not hungry.

Computer Programmer   What about the husband?

Brown-Haired Secretary   He stayed in the street, not
knowing what to do, he didn't go back home and the rain
washed him away.

Computer Programmer   You're making it up, like
everything, as usual.

Brown-Haired Secretary   You know very well I've
never made anything up.

The **Brown-Haired Secretary** *touches her belly*.

Brown-Haired Secretary   Did I make this up as
well?

Computer Programmer   No.

Brown-Haired Secretary   Well, if this is not a
fabrication, everything is possible, believe me, everything is
simple and easy.

Pause.

You haven't told me yet if you like the house.

Computer Programmer   Yes, I like it. Why?

Brown-Haired Secretary   Because . . . nothing.

Computer Programmer   I see.

Pause.

Brown-Haired Secretary   Look.

Computer Programmer   What.

Brown-Haired Secretary   The sun.

For a Complete Catalogue of Methuen Drama titles
write to:

Methuen Drama
Michelin House
81 Fulham Road
London SW3 6RB

Methuen Modern Plays

include work by

Jean Anouilh
John Arden
Margaretta D'Arcy
Peter Barnes
Sebastian Barry
Brendan Behan
Edward Bond
Bertolt Brecht
Howard Brenton
Simon Burke
Jim Cartwright
Caryl Churchill
Noël Coward
Sarah Daniels
Nick Dear
Shelagh Delaney
David Edgar
Dario Fo
Michael Frayn
John Godber
Paul Godfrey
John Guare
Peter Handke
Jonathan Harvey
Iain Heggie
Declan Hughes
Terry Johnson
Barrie Keeffe
Stephen Lowe

Doug Lucie
John McGrath
David Mamet
Patrick Marber
Arthur Miller
Mtwa, Ngema & Simon
Tom Murphy
Phyllis Nagy
Peter Nichols
Joseph O'Connor
Joe Orton
Louise Page
Luigi Pirandello
Stephen Poliakoff
Franca Rame
Philip Ridley
David Rudkin
Willy Russell
Jean-Paul Sartre
Sam Shepard
Wole Soyinka
C. P. Taylor
Theatre de Complicite
Theatre Workshop
Sue Townsend
Judy Upton
Timberlake Wertenbaker
Victoria Wood

Methuen World Classics

Aeschylus (two volumes)
Jean Anouilh
John Arden (two volumes)
Arden & D'Arcy
Aristophanes (two volumes)
Aristophanes & Menander
Peter Barnes (two volumes)
Brendan Behan
Aphra Behn
Edward Bond (four volumes)
Bertolt Brecht
   (five volumes)
Howard Brenton
   (two volumes)
Büchner
Bulgakov
Calderón
Anton Chekhov
Caryl Churchill
   (two volumes)
Noël Coward (five volumes)
Sarah Daniels (two volumes)
Eduardo De Filippo
David Edgar (three volumes)
Euripides (three volumes)
Dario Fo (two volumes)
Michael Frayn (two volumes)
Max Frisch
Gorky
Harley Granville Barker
   (two volumes)
Henrik Ibsen (six volumes)

Terry Johnson
Lorca (three volumes)
David Mamet
Marivaux
Mustapha Matura
David Mercer (two volumes)
Arthur Miller
   (five volumes)
Anthony Minghella
Molière
Tom Murphy
   (three volumes)
Musset
Peter Nichols (two volumes)
Clifford Odets
Joe Orton
Louise Page
A. W. Pinero
Luigi Pirandello
Stephen Poliakoff
   (two volumes)
Terence Rattigan
Ntozake Shange
Sophocles (two volumes)
Wole Soyinka
David Storey (two volumes)
August Strindberg
   (three volumes)
J. M. Synge
Ramón del Valle-Inclán
Frank Wedekind
Oscar Wilde

New titles also available from Methuen

John Godber
Lucky Sods & Passion Killers
0 413 70170 0

Paul Godfrey
A Bucket of Eels & The Modern Husband
0 413 68830 5

Jonathan Harvey
Boom Bang-A-Bang & Rupert Street Lonely Hearts Club
0 413 70450 5

Phyllis Nagy
Weldon Rising & Disappeared
0 413 70150 6

Judy Upton
Bruises & The Shorewatchers' House
0 413 70430 0

Gregory Motton & Elfriede Jelinek
Cat and Mouse (Sheep) & Services
0 413 70760 1

Stig Larsson & Nikolai Kolyada
Sisters, Brothers & The Oginski Polonaise
0 413 70780 6